PRAISE FOR WONDER & BEAUTY

"A truly inspired journey that starts with the deepest kind of heartbreak and ends with the highest form of love beyond limits and healing beyond hopelessness. Charla Miller's book offers example of the exquisite power of intention, solid resolve, and practice. Her willingness to share her very intimate journey gifts us all with evidence of the value of each and every part of our own lives coupled with a beautiful affirmation of humanity's ability to repair and triumph. A warm and thoughtful page-turner, relevant for everyone living, Charla's book gives us illustration of what it is like to hurt, to lose and yet to rise up and to live a powerful vision of love, conscious choice, and hope."

Valerie Valentine, MA, ATR, LPCC, LPAT, CSAT, Art Therapist, Santa Fe, NM

"Charla Miller's captivating story is a testament to the healing power of love, truth and beauty in every woman's search for connection, meaning and wholeness. This beautifully written book, full of heartfelt wisdom and hard won insights, will inspire and support you in never giving up on yourself and your dreams. It is truly a celebration of the resilience of the human spirit."

Pasha Hogan, author of *Third Time Lucky: A Creative Recovery*

"The story you are about to read will inspire you, and help you realize how precious life is and what God has offered you. Find out how the author's fight for survival was made possible by the therapeutic introduction to the equine world. Working with, riding and taking care of horses requires the same acceptance you must have in yourself. Horses, she found, can turn trust and love into acceptance of a human's direction. The author has done this through all the pain and heartache one should not have to endure.

Congratulations Charla; the road you traveled was not easy. Through your work with the horses, and their acceptance, you discovered the beautiful person I always saw. Thank you for sharing your experience."

Elaine Herrlich, equestrian, ret. esthetician, CMT.

"Charla's transparency and willingness to give voice to her struggle paves the way for others to find beauty in the tragedies that block our forward motion. She is a gifted makeup artist with a strong belief in the value of embracing a pro-aging philosophy. What a relief to discover that the loveliness that is her essence is captured in *Wonder and Beauty*. As you read this inspiring book, you will realize that she didn't do the hard work just to release her own healing dialogue; she offers permission and strategies to find your own path to healing."

Lisa Ancira, East Bay Coffee Co.

"Charla brings a very important subject to the table: Presence. When you meet someone who is in touch with her own Presence, it is deeply felt and touches the core of your Being—your own Presence. As Charla points out in her book, most talk therapies don't have the same transforming and healing impact as horse therapy. Animals are in touch with their Presence and horses have a special ability to help transmit that to their 'clients.'

As a Hakomi Therapist, I know how important Presence is for true healing to take place, which is why Charla's insights resonate deeply with me. As a result of her own healing through the Presence of horses, Charla's Presence has become a tangible and healing influence for others."

Pernilla Lillarose, Self-Love Mystic & Mentor, author of *Imagine Being Kind to Yourself.*

WONDER
AND
BEAUTY

MY JOURNEY FROM HEARTBREAK TO HEALING
THROUGH THE WONDER OF HORSES

CHARLA MILLER

BALBOA.
PRESS

A DIVISION OF HAY HOUSE

Copyright © 2016 Charla Miller.

Balboa Press books may be ordered through booksellers or by contacting:

Balboa Press
A Division of Hay House
1663 Liberty Drive
Bloomington, IN 47403
www.balboapress.com
1 (877) 407-4847

Because of the dynamic nature of the Internet, any web addresses or links contained in this book may have changed since publication and may no longer be valid. The views expressed in this work are solely those of the author and do not necessarily reflect the views of the publisher, and the publisher hereby disclaims any responsibility for them.

Print information available on the last page.

ISBN: 978-1-5043-6174-3 (sc)
ISBN: 978-1-5043-6176-7 (hc)
ISBN: 978-1-5043-6175-0 (e)

Library of Congress Control Number: 2016910949

Balboa Press rev. date: 10/12/2016

DISCLAIMER

This is a work of creative nonfiction. The book's content is a compilation of thoughts, memories, and feelings experienced by the author. This is her personal recollection of events that occurred and that led up to the writing of this book. While some folks may challenge the accuracy of the facts, the facts, as written, are as the author remembers them. While all the stories in this book are true, some names and identifying details have been changed to protect the privacy of the people involved.

To God, the Divine source of healing power and love for all of us. Thank you for showing yourself to me in the most surprising ways.

CONTENTS

FOREWORD
BY DR. NANCY FREITAS LAMBERT, PsyD

I first met Charla on Sept 1, 2012, when she arrived for a women's "Creating Intimacy" Equine Therapy Group. When I saw Charla get out of her car, I was immediately struck by her physical beauty and the direct and purposeful way she moved, and also, the competence that each movement displayed. I instantly knew that no matter what she had endured in her life, this woman was a survivor.

She began explaining a bit about her life and her current situation, and as she spoke she became more and more agitated by the minute; she seemed confused and filled with rage and anger. I knew our journey with the horses was going to be about creating a safe and sacred place for Charla. A place where she could start to uncover her grief and sorrow, and a place where she could begin to find a way back to her true authentic self. I truly hoped the horses would help her find a path that would lead her back to her soul.

So, we began our journey—courageous, stunning Charla, the beautiful horses, and I. Charla spent a great deal of time with the horses. She bonded and connected and showed incredible courage and resolve, facing her unthinkable grief and sorrow. She had an extremely close connection with one of the mares in the herd. It was through her willingness to begin to trust this mare, and depend on the strength and presence of the horses, that she found her way back to herself. With tremendous grace and beauty, Charla was able to face the emotional turmoil she had suffered in her life. She was able to find the hope, strength, and courage she needed to go on. Her story is a true gift to us all. She is a true inspiration to me. As she continues to face her fears and move forward through her life, she reminds me that we all need an opportunity to heal and be true to ourselves, no matter what.

As Charla's bittersweet journey of healing continues, she has made a decision to share her story for the sole purpose of offering others a way to remain hopeful and have faith, even in our darkest times.

For the past sixteen years, I have been treating people who have a history of trauma, and I specialize in working with women who have suffered profound loss and survived traumatic events. What I see most often in the experience of trauma, is women who have been psychologically forced to unintentionally abandon their true selves in order to survive. They have lost touch with the unique aspects of themselves. It is this survival process of dissociation that helps women in their deepest need for protection, yet also robs them of a truly integrated life experience.

Trauma survivors need the opportunity to feel safe enough to get curious about their lost self, about their innocence, about their dreams and their passion, about *their* life. They need to become willing to face their demons—their false beliefs and perceptions about the world, others, and themselves. They have to feel safe enough to grieve and they have to learn to trust again.

I feel blessed to have been a witness to the courageous and graceful healing process Charla experienced—her loving journey back to herself—and her willingness to honor and trust the horses and follow them as they guided her where she needed to go. I am forever grateful.

Nancy Freitas Lambert, PsyD, Founder of Wonder Equine Therapy

INVOCATION

For all the mothers, fathers, and family members who have been affected by the senseless and painful separation from their children, I've written this for you.

I've heard your comments and I thank you for your support for the work I've done to reconnect with my son. I've followed your heart-wrenching stories of heroism to reconnect with your children, and your journeys have encouraged me in the most profound and positive ways. For your courage and perseverance, I thank you from the depths of my being.

Our children, no matter where they are, can feel our love as well as our pain. Our greatest enemy is hopelessness.

My message for you is one of reunion in the here and now. I've come to believe and know this is possible. To live in harmony with our children is our right and theirs. All children have a right to know they are loved and in the realm of spirit this is always possible.

They feel us and they know our hearts as we know theirs. They want us to be happy and free, and in this state the probability of reunion exists.

My desire for you, wherever you are on your path of connection and healing, is to know that the next step will present itself and lead you to love's door. The day will come when our heavenly reunion will take place, whether in this realm or the next. Take comfort in this belief.

CHAPTER 1

THE TOUCH OF HEALING

God made great doctors for healing the body, but he made
the horse for healing the soul.
—Author unknown

The birth of my healing came about in the most unusual and surprising way. My first session with my therapist came to a close and we were putting the horses away. We closed the gate and I took one more look at May, the mare, and put my fingers through the fence to reach for her. May gently pressed back on my fingers and in this silent moment her message to me was firm. This was my first personal communication with her and it was crystal clear: *You are finally safe now.*

My name is Charla Miller. I am a mother, sister, friend and partner. I became a writer so I could give voice to the power of the human spirit and the indomitable love for my child. This memoir was prompted by years of court cases and the final abduction of my son. My story isn't one of revenge but of reclaiming myself through this heartbreak. Through *God's* grace and *Divine* love I discovered the healing power of horses, and with the compassionate care of a

1

doctor and her herd I grew to believe in my ability to heal from this atrocity. The horses walked me into emotional and psychological places I would not dare to go, and one specific horse, named May, encouraged me to journey into the most painful experience of my life and recognize that I could survive it and stand tall in my truth.

I had sought many different therapeutic answers for myself, knowing instinctively if I didn't, I would be lost in the abyss of no return. Four years earlier, in 2007, I had been on the edge of that abyss. The hundreds of lawsuits my ex-husband had filed against me over every imaginable (and unimaginable) detail of the custody of our son, both factual and fictional, had placed me in a dire emotional and financial state. This went on in a full-court-press manner until 2009. In that period of time, my dad, who was my one and only protector in life, passed away, and my ex-husband knew it was his time to take full advantage and make good on his promise to "destroy" me.

There had been several abductions of my son at this point, but I had always gotten him back. I was tattered, weary, and just plain tortured from seven years of post-divorce war. It was the "perfect storm," and I couldn't keep it together anymore. The foreclosures in the real estate market in 2008 had begun and we were caught in that first wave.

My son and I had returned from a much-needed weekend away with friends and as I walked up to our home I saw a letter of eviction taped to the door. That letter felt like the last nail in the coffin to me. I couldn't hide within our shelter and keep the world out any longer. Our home was being taken away and this last devastation was just too much for me. I had never in my life been without a home of my own, even if it was a small and humble apartment. I felt like a failure as a mother and the sole protector and provider of my son. I had enough cash left to get an apartment, but because of the pending foreclosure and my business demise (I was a real estate professional), I no longer had the mental or emotional reserves to figure out our next move to meet our basic needs.

The prior years and circumstances had me in a state of constant hypervigilance and my mind never stopped trying to work out how to save us. There were some uninterrupted nights of sleep, but they never long enough to escape the relentless planning for either the current custody battle or the next attack from the banks and identity thieves.

I used to watch countless films on boxers and warriors in battle. I watched films like *Braveheart*, the *Rocky* films, and others that depicted fighters with a heart and mission to survive. I watched in the hopes that I could glean some hidden secret to winning the war I was in. But the day had now come when I knew I would have to stop fighting for everything, including my right to co-parent and be with my son.

The thought of letting my son go was more painful than the thought of amputating one of my limbs. It felt as if it would shred every cell of my being. But in the midst of this impending darkness, I continued to hear the whisper of my spirit—*never give up*. I heard the message but I didn't know how to not give up on me, while I had to give up on us. This new identity of mother without her child went against every primal instinct. The thought of living my life without my son was incomprehensible.

The eviction letter from the bank included instructions to leave the house intact and not vandalized. It also came with an offer called "cash for keys," where the bank would give me a couple thousand dollars if I complied with their instructions. I was never a messy person and certainly never thought of vandalizing any place I lived in. But these were desperate times, and anger and uncertainty were rampant. I saw many homes with torn-out kitchens and even toilets gone. Graffiti was painted all over the insides of once-beautiful homes. I had witnessed the anger-fueled damage in these houses as a real estate salesperson. The actions of fearful people fed the fears that were growing within me.

At that point in the foreclosure process, the money being offered to me seemed like the best choice I could make in the face of the overwhelming wave of trouble that was heading toward me. I had thirty days to leave my home. In that period of time I needed to clean, pack, and give away things I couldn't take with me to my next place. I did all of this while dealing with another frivolous lawsuit brought by my ex-husband and his girlfriend. I felt as if I were in a surging ocean. I now realize I am thankful I had experienced the feeling of being in a turbulent ocean because I learned how to anticipate the waves, when to take a deep breath and duck under them. Every time I came up on the other side of a wave, I barely had enough time to take a breath before the next wave came barreling down on me.

Several years later the bank that took my home was found guilty of fraud in a major class action suit brought on by millions of foreclosed homeowners. I received a check and almost threw it away thinking it was junk mail. I was shocked to see that the bank had lost the class action lawsuit. As a homeowner who had been foreclosed on fraudulently, I received a check in the amount of $315. My initial investment in the home had been $75,000. How ironic, and yet another lesson in learning to let go.

Transformation of any kind isn't easy and the path before me looked like the moon, desolate and quiet. I traversed this new landscape with the belongings I had and pondered my options as to where to go and what I could do to support myself. I chose to travel five hundred miles away, to the birthplace of my son. In the middle of the financial crash, I knew the San Francisco Bay Area had a better economy, and I heard the call to go back to seek the answers I desperately needed. I'm the kind of woman who wants to understand why and how something could have gone so wrong. I wanted to know how to fix it, to fix me and make it good again, like it had been or at least how I perceived it once was. I was still operating on my logic and desire to control my life, but as I became more willing to move forward, the road ahead revealed itself step by step, breath by breath. My vision and daily goal was one of peace and having enough to get through that day. I had come to see that logic had little to do with the unfolding road ahead.

I had friends in Northern California that I kept in touch with. They knew every grave detail of my unraveling, and I called them as I drove north and they insisted I come to their home for as long as I needed. To go back to the place of my son's birth might have furthered the local rumors about my state of mind, but something bigger than all of this knew I needed to begin there again. I needed to remember the days of my dreams realized as a mother and proud wife, and the joys I had known and deeply felt. I needed to try to make sense of the choices I had made and move on to make new choices, just for myself. I began the unfathomable acceptance of my new reality—that I would not, could not, be with my son if I were to have any chance of survival. I would have to go it alone, for now.

I drove north in a daze knowing I wouldn't return. I remembered the envelope my dear friend had given me. I had stuffed it in my purse and forgotten about it until I stopped for gas and a bathroom break. My car was packed to the gills. My once-fancy Mercedes was now an even more important vehicle. I owned it outright and it was my home and shelter until I reached my next stop in Marin, California. I left with four hundred dollars I had made at a garage sale the day before, and that unopened envelope. Before I started to drive I opened the envelope and inside was a check for several thousand dollars. That wasn't just money I needed desperately; I saw it as tangible evidence of God giving me a fully inflated life raft, assuring me I could breathe and begin to relax just a bit.

With the gift of cash from my friend and a home to live in for a while, I ventured north to search for the answers I needed. Northern California was filled with memories of many life-altering events: My wedding and marriage. My son's birth. The purchase of our beautiful home and our many parties and social gatherings with family and friends.

I had known a great and fruitful life in Northern California, and I believe my soul knew I had to prove and see for myself that my life had been happy, loving, and kind. I had been the co-creator in that dream once, and if I ventured back to that place and time I would see that it had been good. I would see that even though I was walking through the ashes of my life now I could begin again, and a new world would unfold for me. This thought became my new vision for myself, and it always included the dream of having my son in it as well.

After I was settled in my friends' son's room, and his bunk bed had become my new safe haven, I had the burning desire to visit the home in which my son was raised. I was a few miles away from the memories of his early years, and though the thought of seeing my beautiful home seemed like a crazy idea, I knew I had to physically view it again.

I drove to our former home on a very peaceful street in Marin California. As I sat in my car looking at it for the first time in years, everything became hushed. I couldn't feel if the temperature was hot or cold. I didn't care if the neighbors saw or recognized me. I needed confirmation that what I had experienced there was *real*. It was a defining moment for me. I was alive and I could, and would walk on from here.

I needed to give my mind time to unscramble the past events and my spirit needed the space and quiet to begin to heal from all the loss and tragedy. As I stared at my former home, I acknowledged there was no room for any more blame; just a quiet knowing of what had been and that it was good. Now I could begin to recreate my life as a single woman with more focus than I had ever had for anything before.

It was in the San Francisco Bay Area that I first felt the power of the *Touch of Healing*. My son gave me that gift in a second. He was born by cesarean section so it was impossible to hold him, but the doctors told his father to bring him to me and hold his little cheek against mine while they took care of me. The moment I felt his flesh, his face, and his spirit, I was transformed. All of my past hurts, longings, and misunderstandings vanished instantly. That was the most pivotal moment in my life and it described just how powerful one touch can be. I could never have imagined what was waiting for me in another transformative touch. This time, this touch wouldn't be with a human but with a mythic animal, a beautiful mare named May.

Reflections: The Touch of Healing

Healing requires a willingness to be open and vulnerable and this is counterintuitive to a survivor of trauma. This tragedy gave me an opportunity to find a new path to journey on.

I've met those who could not face their story be tempered in fire and walk out of it to begin again. I learned from their example that only I could choose to heal from this and rewrite the ending of my story.

I would make many changes in order to heal and I learned I'd have to explore my interior world to get beyond an ocean of suffering. I no longer could stand the pain of *just* surviving and retelling the stories from my past. I had to find the way of rebirth.

I became single-minded in learning about the indomitable spirit of the soul and to find out if I possessed that same spirit.

My quest invited me to hear God's whispers in new ways through the introduction of communicating with horses. I was being taught the power of staying present in the moment by these animals and this was the primary act that helped me to get out of my story.

I no longer feel alone on my healing path, nor do I feel like I'm the outside observer to life anymore. I've become curious and connected to my ancestors and to their stories of hardships and losses. I've connected with family members that I'd never met before this tragedy and we now engage with each other in ways I never dreamed possible. I believe all who have crossed my path in my healing journey are cheering me on, those who have passed on and those who are still here. I feel their spirit in my life every day.

To heal, you have to believe, so I began with a mustard-seed size of faith that my daily needs would be provided. I grew to trust that God, the *Divine*, the Love that created me, would fulfill those needs. These are food, shelter, safety, and companionship. Whatever else I didn't have was no longer important.

I began with this question: *Do I have what I need for today? Do I have a safe place to stay, food, work, and maybe the support of a friend around me?* If my answers were yes, and most of the time they were, I began to feel a change in me. I felt more grounded and my appreciation grew. This allowed me to begin healing the losses, and hearing more clearly what I needed to do next. This calm comes from the belief that in the present I am okay and I have what I need right now. The practice of being present grows gratitude and thus has brought me the richness in life that I experience today.

I have faith in each moment there will be a place for you to rest, nutritious food to eat, and comfort for you in the most unlikely places, and with the most surprising of companions, if you too choose to walk on. When you see an unopened door, don't be afraid to open it wide. There is more waiting for you on the other side of it.

CHAPTER 2

YELLOW ROSE ON THE BRIDGE

We can only be what we give ourselves the power to be.
—Chief Meninock in Joyce Hifler,
A Cherokee Feast of Days: Daily Meditations

I arrived in San Francisco, the birthplace of my son. The birth of a child is a turning point in a woman's life, and those memories last a lifetime. I had returned, not to give birth to a child, but to myself. Even though from the outside it might have looked as if I was running away from my life, I was in fact putting distance between myself and my ex-spouse and his campaign to destroy me. My spirit knew what I needed and that was to reclaim my life. I started the drive from Southern California in the morning, and by the time I arrived I had been driving for ten hours. It was the first time in years I had been back to Northern California, and my decision to leave my home, near my son, had been the most tormented one of my life.

I arrived looking worn and feeling jolted from the ride. But with the first breath I took of the sweet Northern California air, I was able to distance myself from my past. It was an incredible relief. It was a surreal time to be back with my friend Kathryn and her family. They knew the story of my son's abduction, and have always been the one family to give us support, comfort, and care throughout the years. I met Kathryn in a moms group in Marin ten years prior. On the long drive back to San Francisco, I had reminisced about the years spent raising my son and all the family gatherings, outings in the redwoods, s'mores we made by the campfires, and the good times in our safe little mommies group. My mind was in a constant loop, replaying the minute details of my life with my son, recalling memories that only he and I shared. It seemed too much of a leap in life for me to be back where my life as a mother began. And now I was without my child.

Kathryn gave me a place to sleep in her little boy's room in his extra bunk bed. His art, toys, and clothes were everywhere. To be reminded of my son when he had been her youngest child's age was comforting. For short periods, I could lose myself in good memories. But returning to the present was confusing and painful. My mind would wander back to our life in Marin, and how I had considered myself to be a loving wife and mother. I lavished care on our son, our home, and our marriage, striving for perfection. And now I was in my friend's son's room in the extra bunk bed, without a son, a home, or a job.

Throughout my life I've always made sense out of any rough patch by writing to-do lists and completing them as soon as humanly possible. Now I was living out of a suitcase and sharing a bathroom with an entire family. Even though they welcomed me, I knew I needed a place of my own, even if it was just a private bedroom. I also needed an income and a reason to wake up every day and convince myself to keep on breathing. One lesson I had learned as a child was to never wear out my welcome, so I was highly motivated.

It was Christmas time and I knew the shops that I had frequented as an affluent Marin shopper would be hiring holiday help. So I created an updated résumé on my friend's computer. Then I pulled out the best outfit I had, drove to the mall, and dropped off my résumé at several stores. After that, I would take my turn on my friend's computer every day and go straight to Craigslist. The first thing I looked for was a room to rent. As much as I was comforted by being around my friends and any level of familiarity, I needed a room so I could let out my painful emotions. I wasn't used to this ugly and often out-of-control side of myself. When waves of grief washed over me, I wanted nothing more than to disappear. But I knew I would have to keep masking my devastation with makeup and nice clothes. I had to fool the outside world into believing that I was fine. After many years of defeat, my soul was longing for victory. I needed to know that every day I was moving in a positive direction.

After six days in Northern California, I had my three basic needs met: a room (with a view), a job, and the companionship of my landlady from time to time. Just knowing that she was around was comfort beyond belief and it helped keep me from sliding back into the darkness of despair. That winter was one of the coldest and wettest winters on record, which mirrored my life at that time.

I had always had a strong work ethic; at fourteen I had my first job in a pizza place. But this job and the chance to start over would bring even more of an awareness of the value of hard work, money, and time. It's one thing to be a teen working at an entry-level job and quite another to have the same kind of job in your fifties. But after the 2008 housing and financial crash, I was in the company of many people in their fifties and sixties who were starting over and willing to wear a mask of contentment and take home any kind of paycheck. I've always been eager to learn and liked to do my work quickly, and this lifelong trait served me well now.

I wanted to start other positive practices, so I looked for something around me that was beautiful to help me manage the rough emotions and reality of my circumstances. It seemed that every time I went outside, I would find examples of soothing beauty. Slowly I learned that when I paid attention to the stunning landscape around me, my grief, fear, and loneliness would loosen their grip on me.

My private bedroom, in an exclusive area of Marin, had a large wooden deck overlooking the woods and the San Francisco Bay. When I gazed out my window in the mornings, I could see the tankers and ships sailing by, with the outline of the city of San Francisco in the background. The city looked like a queen's crown sitting on top of one of the prettiest bays in the world. I knew that something much bigger than myself had been working on my behalf to find me the most perfect room and circumstances, at a price I could afford, at a time when I truly needed it.

The peace of my new home was almost overwhelming. After more than a decade of chaos, I felt my world slowing down. I stopped feeling that I was hanging on for dear life. For the first time since my home had been foreclosed on and I had admitted defeat in the custody battles, I felt a sense of calm. I even felt that one day I might be able to break free of the bitterness, pain, and terror of my past. This thought had seemed utterly impossible in the years prior, but being back in Marin, I was looking at my life from a broader perspective, to imagine viewing my life without the story.

I began to venture out in my new neighborhood. I took walks and appreciated the view as I breathed in the fresh air and feeling of freedom. I encountered deer and raccoons, and they didn't run away from me. The peace I was experiencing was helping me feel kind and gentle—and normal—again. As I took this time to settle into my new home I had an amazing kitchen to inspire me. I was operating on a small budget for all of my basic needs, but the grand view from this kitchen made my humble meals of rice, beans, and vegetables feel like a gourmet meals. I made every effort to be mindful that I lived in one of the most affluent and scenic places in the world, and even though I was starting over at rock bottom there must have been some reason I was led there. And out of all the people that called on the listing I was the person this room was rented to. Every night before I went to sleep I saw the Golden Gate

Bridge and remembered the story of how it was built despite all the obstacles it faced. In the moonlight of the evening the story of the bridge inspired me and I felt comforted in the hope that I too could build a life worth living.

I had been hired by a local home designer company, where I sold luxury home furnishings. This job allowed me to feel as if I had a beautiful home again. In the evenings I had my room to retreat to, to cry and thaw out my feelings of fear, heartache, and sorrow. At that time, I had very little experience expressing grief or shame. I studied my emotions and came to understand how self-destructive they could be, how they made me feel as if I had a weight tied to my feet while I was treading water, with my face bobbing up and down. I was just hoping not to drown.

The year before I left my home and drove back to Marin, a friend had given me a weeklong course at Esalen called Gifts of Grief. Ten other people from all over the world took the class with me. Many of their stories were about the loss of a loved one through death; one woman had lost her son to suicide. I related to her the most because she looked like she carried so much guilt over her son's loss. Before the course on grief, most of what I had observed of loss and pain had been shrouded in secrecy, which masqueraded as privacy. I was alone in trying to make sense out of my feelings. Also, I wasn't grieving a death. If I had been, I would have gotten sympathy cards. Instead, I was grieving the loss of my stolen child, which had occurred in my own country, in my own state, in *my* town. I had gotten little support for this loss; instead, I received shaming glances and remarks from those who did not know what had happened.

Brené Brown, PhD, LMSW, writes and teaches on the subjects of shame and vulnerability. I read her book, *The Gifts of Imperfection,* and it deepened my insight into the pressure I had put on myself when it came to the loss of my son. I needed an explanation of what I was feeling, and I also needed ways to grieve his loss and to change my identity as his mother. Though I was still his mother, I was no longer in his life. It seemed like an impossible task to address these subjects without sinking into a deeper depression, but to my surprise I found myself feeling lighter. My darkness was fading.

At the end of my stay at Esalen, I found myself laughing with a woman who had lost her husband, her soul mate, and we both hadn't laughed that hard for a very long time. It was like a dam had broken and we allowed ourselves to be human in all the messy complexities of grief.

But I had many years to go before I could put pen to paper and write about my loss without feeling that the pain and hurt would consume me. I first had to have a place to mourn these losses, and accept that the mystery of where my son was and how he was doing would be my new reality.

I believe God gave me the perfect place to begin this part of my healing. The private room I found had been on Craigslist for only thirty minutes when I called and spoke with the woman who would became my friend and landlady for the next year. I had landed in a place of peace and beauty, and I experienced the kind of quiet one finds after a huge storm or traumatic event passes. I had the clear sense that something tremendous was over and the next phase of my life was about to begin.

At this point I decided to get outdoors and exercise again. I hiked with the fervor of a woman who was shedding the nightmares of her past. I took trails that I had never known existed. One day I hiked straight up a mountain and when I reached the top of the trail I couldn't believe what I was seeing. I was looking out over the entire San Francisco Bay Area! I felt free. For the first time in years, a sense of empowerment returned to me, like a familiar, kind friend. My mantra—one breath at a time—had taken me to the most incredible view of San Francisco, which was the birthplace of my son and the place where my spirit was being reborn.

One morning I woke up in the middle of a winter storm with an intense desire to drive to the Golden Gate Bridge and walk across it. This idea tested my feeling of security, as I hadn't ventured far from where I was living, especially during a storm. At this point I had a job and a daily schedule, and this gave me more self-confidence and a growing feeling of stability. I needed to get to the bridge and return, shower, and get to work all in a matter of a few hours. I drove to the bridge and parked my car on its west side. I crossed under the bridge to get to the east side, where the walking path was, and felt the wind, the cold, and the light rain. I became overwhelmed. Along with my new mantras, which helped me through waves of grief and emotional pain, I had also adopted a practice of carrying something with me to redirect my mind away from negativity and toward more positive thoughts.

That morning I had brought a dried yellow rose from a bouquet I had received. I no longer threw things away, as I might have in the past. Now every gift and gesture was used and appreciated in ways I had never imagined before. The yellow rose in the bouquet was matched by a painting of a blooming yellow rose I had brought with me from Southern California. The painting had been given to me as partial payment from a woman I had helped hold a garage sale. The painting was exquisite—a yellow rose perfectly blossomed and opened to life. There was something about this painting that resonated with me. It had not sold at the garage sale, and I'd not been able to take my eyes off its simplicity and perfection. So when it came time to pay me my share of the profits, I asked for the painting in lieu of some of my pay. The next day, I took my four hundred dollars and my painting of a yellow rose and drove away. I still have that painting today as a reminder of my life and how it has unfolded, not without pain or trials, but with beauty.

That day on the bridge, I had on my warmest down jacket, hat, gloves, and scarf. Inside all of the layers, next to my heart, was the dried yellow rose. Many times on my journey I'd get very clear instructions from a voice or whisper inside of me. The voice, which often was a strong feeling, would guide me. All I needed to do was listen, pay attention, and carry out the instructions.

It seemed odd to bring this rose with me on my walk over the Golden Gate Bridge on this stormy day. I walked briskly onto the bridge, warming up and feeling invigorated. I came around one of the bright reddish-orange monolithic spires and was almost swept away by a gust of wind. This was both frightening and enlivening; I was completely present and alert. I approached the midsection of the bridge and saw a loose wire attached to a spire. I had the thought to stop and tie my dried yellow rose to the bridge and secure it with the help of this random wire. I took off my gloves and my hands went almost numb, but I positioned myself to break some of the gusts of wind and carried out the instruction that was given to me.

Once I tied the rose to the bridge, I understood why I had come. This was a *Divine* moment for me on my path. I looked at the dried yellow rose secured to the bridge and made a promise to myself. Like the rose, I had gone dry and was weathering a bitter storm. But just as I had tethered the rose securely to that iconic bridge, I too had been given a place to tether myself to until the next move was revealed. I took out my cell phone and shot a video of that rose and spoke these words into the phone: *From this day forward, I'll carry myself across any bridge of life I need to cross. I'll bear the difficulties of my path, and I will never give up on my love for my son. Somehow I will find a way to communicate this to him.*

I made those promises to myself and my son in that storm, and those promises have remained a part of my life to this day. The thornier part of my promise would be to forgive myself and believe that I am and have always been worth loving.

Just as a room, a job, and companionship had come to me, so too would the continuing support and care for my next steps. The next *Divine* appointment would take place in a faraway pasture in Point Reyes Station, California, surrounded by awe-inspiring creatures called horses.

Reflections: Yellow Rose on the Bridge

I felt lifeless and my circumstances seemed impossible. Waiting and resting in the silence, I found my next steps and secrets for carrying on.

Just as water flows from a stream to the ocean, your ability to get beyond the hardest circumstances of your life already exists. Your willingness to keep walking through the storms of life will eventually take you to the right places, people, and circumstances that will inspire you to a greater reality.

You can only be what you give yourself the power to be and maybe all you can do at first is give yourself the permission to stop and rest. But eventually you will see the right path to take and the right support will come. From these actions hope will grow. And with hope, it will become clear that you can reclaim a better life.

What is the best thing you can do today to rest? What single task can you do to make headway in improving your work life, your home environment, and your health? Every time you finish a step to improve one of these you exercise your strength. Making loving choices for yourself becomes a testament to the power to change your life.

CHAPTER 3

THE POWER OF WONDER

*Why do you stay in prison when the door
is so wide open?*
—Rumi

Many times I wondered, Would I make it through all of this? Oddly enough, it was my sense of wonder that saved me.

I learned that healing from trauma is not an A to Z process, or at least it wasn't for me. What I wanted was a straight line, with the assurance of a positive outcome. Whenever I felt that my journey was linear and predictable, I would feel myself calm down. By the time I started to work on the trauma of the past, I had already been through more than a half dozen types of therapy, including past-life regression, cognitive therapy with several intuitive therapists, family constellation classes, and psychiatry, which involved pharmaceuticals for depression. But talking in groups or in one-on-one therapy only took the edge off my pain, and the pharmaceuticals ultimately were of little use and even a danger to me. I was once given a prescribed dose of medication for my depression and I nearly passed out from it. This revealed something about myself that I had always suspected, that I was a much more sensitive person in every way. When I took a medication it acted more strongly on me than it was supposed to. I also felt things deeply, especially other people's emotions, and I always had an intuition about what might be best for my own well-being. But I didn't trust this. Many times throughout my life I chose to ignore my intuition and dismiss my inner promptings. I allowed other people's opinions to dictate my way of healing instead of honoring the voice inside that came from my intuitive nature. I, like so many women, looked for support in relationships and families that just didn't or couldn't give it. I knew I needed to build self-confidence and believe in myself so I looked for it outside myself. I wanted permission from the world so I wouldn't make any more mistakes. I was terrified that the other shoe was already dropping. To me, if someone gave me support it was the same as giving me permission to heal with the guarantee that I would be okay.

Before I left for Northern California, the best advice I received, from a highly respected physician and therapist, was to pack my belongings, leave the area, and start my life over again. She feared that something would happen to me as I had not yet given up on my parental right to be with my son. She knew there would be no reprieve for me until I gave up and moved away. Thus my health had no way to improve until I made the choice to surrender and give myself a chance to heal somewhere else. I trusted her and listened to her advice and at this point that was rare. My doctor was right, and it wasn't through a prescription that I started healing, it was through the truth.

Answers to my questions about how to heal came in many different forms. One night I went to a group therapy session that I had never attended before. All during that day I debated going, but it was as if an outside force was leading me there. I arrived and sat in the inner circle. I listened to a young man talk about his mother and the fact that she had committed suicide.

That caught my attention, so I turned around to look at him. When I saw him, I thought he looked the way my son might look twenty years in the future, and it shocked me! His skin and hair color looked like my son's and he had a similar build. He spoke with a low voice, and he appeared fragile yet physically strong. He was devastated by his mother's death, and just like myself was in a sea of people—hurting, confused, yet living with the pain. I turned back around and faced forward so that one fewer pair of eyes was watching him and just listened. During his talk I knew without a doubt that I had been led there that night and placed in front of him, to give me a glance into my son's and my future. I realized that night that no matter what I would have to go through from that point forward, I would not leave my son in that manner.

I contemplated the meaning of leaving a legacy. The word legacy was never a word I heard growing up, but in this moment I understood everyone leaves one and I wondered what I wanted to leave. This made me stop and think about my life in a way I had never done before. Until this point, I had been reacting solely out of fear and life circumstances. I had to practice being present in the moment and choosing my actions based on the circumstances right now. The practice of being present was foreign and not easy to remember in the beginning, and even today this mindset takes practice.

I wanted to become less reactionary and I made a decision that I would not leave my son with the legacy that his mother ended her life in defeat in any manner. I understood how deeply someone's action affects others and how it left a lifetime of sorrow for that young man to sort through. When he was speaking I felt that I was the intended recipient of his mother's story, and I was given the chance to honor her life by living mine.

Throughout this journey I was drawn to exploring churches, not just because of their beauty, but also because of my belief in their sacred power to heal people. Throughout my life I often sought out and visited them. Most of the time, I felt comfort and peace.

Being in a church was familiar to me—I was raised in a Christian family and activities that centered on the church were part of my history. I have many memories of weddings and family gatherings, and consider myself fortunate to have had this introduction to a church community. However, there have also been times I've felt a profound connection with the *Divine* that had very little to do with the community.

When I stepped inside a church, I often had the experience of feeling what the church might be feeling when people came to pray with their petitions, sorrows, and gratitude. It's as if the church was a great big person and let me into its heart, and showed me how it felt inside and how it felt about the people that came for its comfort. This had become an intimate and timeless relationship to me with no misunderstanding because of the religion of the church. This relationship with churches gave me an inescapable sense of wonder.

The small groups I participated in through church helped me to work through a portion of my pain, but there always came a time that I felt I had gone as far as I could go in this kind of community. The grief I was carrying inside became too much for me to fake a smile on Sundays, so I eventually ended up isolating myself again and continued to seek different paths.

Looking back now, it wasn't that I didn't fit in or that I had failed my church experience, it was more that my spirit knew there was more to learn and it was time to travel on. The growth of my soul required more letting go of preconceived ideas about healing and the right or wrong way to wholeness. I was aware this was essential in order for the next step to reveal itself.

Silence became my next church. In that silence I could receive and trust my inner callings. In that silence I began to feel the *Divine* without the sermons and schedules. Silence on my walks became the most natural way for me to be in communion with *Spirit* and feel in harmony with the world around me. My trust continued to grow and even though my life on the outside may have looked like my losses were too great, I knew I was beginning to heal.

All conventional methods of healing my life had been exhausted. As a mother of a child who was stolen and alienated from me, I found no doctor, therapist, or group of any kind could give me the insight I was looking for. And no court, attorney, or police department could make this injustice right. Parent alienation is a result of one parent who has a mission to keep the child away from the other parent. The greatest harm happens to the child of this unlawful separation. Hate and fear are the motives for the alienating parent and, with enough resources, that parent can be successful in the twisting of the mind of the child, and eventually the child as a whole.

Having acknowledged these facts and surrendered to this reality, I became single-minded in seeking out clues that would bring me to a state of calm. I had very few resources at this point, so the library became my best friend for entertainment as well as therapy. I took full advantage of the film section and one day came upon the subject that captured my attention and had entertained me decades ago—horses.

This subject of horse films was a magnet for me just as the films that portrayed fighters and their relentless quest for survival was before. These films were on a nonstop loop in my home like a movie I hoped to blend into. Every time I walked past the screen and caught a glimpse of the film, I imagined myself free, safe, and content with life, just like the horses were. I trusted my intuition more and believed that I could learn a lesson if it was presented in a compassionate way. I knew *God* was revealing this truth through films about horses. Just as before, there came a time when the *Divine* opened another door of thought for me and showed me that I had learned how to survive, and I could go ahead and check off that box. That lesson was complete. I never could have guessed where this path would take me, or that my next teacher would be in the form of a horse.

I had been seeking hope and freedom and horses became that symbol for me. They gave me a new way to see myself and my life forever. My first therapeutic horse film was *Secretariat.* This is the story about a racehorse that did the *inconceivable* in horse-racing history. Secretariat won the Triple Crown in 1973, and in his last race of the crown won the Belmont Stakes by 31 lengths! To this day his record is unbeaten and he is still considered a phenomenon in the history of horse racing. I know this story came into my life right at the time I needed something supernatural to believe in. The film of Secretariat's story paved new pathways for my brain to see other ways to live. There were times in the film I felt I was the horse being trained by my circumstances to do the inconceivable. The message wasn't one of survival anymore; it was one of having the freedom to run your race.

I lived this concept of against all odds for years, and now I hungered to live my life and beat the odds of my past. I wanted to do the inconceivable, just as Secretariat had done.

The story of Secretariat and his owner Penny Tweedy resonated with me. I was in training to live my life differently and change my role as a mother who went missing. Just as Penny Tweedy was becoming independent of her sole role as mother and wife in a generation that didn't accept this, I was becoming acceptable again to myself as my son's mother. She was finding her power in a world of a male-dominated sport and time, and I was finding mine after leaving a life of being dominated. I had power just as Secretariat had and if I wanted to become a winner I knew I'd have to allow others to support me. This made me step out of my isolation and be open to gaining support from others. Just as Secretariat's team made him the winner of the Triple Crown, I let myself be open to finding my own team. I wanted to go the distance now and I never imagined that the inspiration to do this would come from a film about a racehorse.

I watched the film dozens of times and studied Penny Tweedy's passion, commitment to her family's legacy, and love for Secretariat. All of these factors made the story of Secretariat immortal. Penny Tweedy continued to talk about and promote the story of her horse long after he had passed away until Disney Studios made a film about it. Her passion and love for her horse never wavered, and just as she went on to talk about her horse I would continue to talk about my love for my son. Every time I watched the film I became a little stronger in my mind and my health continued to improve.

If I was to win in my life again and become my best self, I would have to learn to be vulnerable and to trust again. I would have to imagine having a community and team around me and allow their support in my life.

Following my soul's longing for restoration hadn't been easy to do. I didn't always know why I had a burning desire to watch this film, but after learning about how our brains can make new neural pathways, and recognizing the need for connection, it made sense to watch this film over and over again. It had all of the components of love, connection, support, and victory in it.

The ache of longing and of belonging has always been part of my life experience. My overwhelming desire for a healed heart and a life rich with all of these pieces had become my number one priority. I knew I had the opportunity to be much more than just a survivor. I pictured Secretariat in the pasture grazing and with that image my soul's true nature unveiled itself as indomitable and free. I got it! I was integrating the spirit of a Triple Crown horse and his nature into mine.

I searched the Internet using terms such as horses, emotional healing, and compassionate care. This search revealed the world of equine therapy—a way to heal through relationships with horses.

I spent hours reading stories about humans and horses. In my research I found a film called *Buck*, the story of a man named Buck Brannaman. At a young age he and his brother were taken out of their home and put into a loving foster-care home. Many years later when Buck is introduced to one of the top horse trainers of that time, Roy Hunt, Buck is captivated by the relationship that Roy Hunt had with his horse and his ability to make an untrained horse do, almost effortlessly, what he wanted it to do. He overcame his past and took his passion for working with horses and made it his profession. His interest in horses helped him heal from his past and now he presents horse clinics all over the country. The relationship with his horse was one of trust and vulnerability and was a profound experience for Buck, as it was for me while I watched. I was swept away in wonder. Buck's story about healing from childhood abuse was my answer.

Being with these animals of grace and wonder had all of the components to not just capture my attention, but to introduce me to a whole other way of being present in my life. Even though horses weigh on average upward of a thousand pounds and their spirit can be unpredictable, I have had the most profound emotional healing with them. When I look into the eyes of a horse, and that look is returned, there is an engagement. By working with horses I began to trust myself in ways that initially felt foreign but truly life-affirming.

Through my research into equine therapy, I spoke with several equine therapists on the phone. One day a conversation with a therapist led to my meeting Nancy Freitas Lambert, PsyD. My sense of wonder turned into an irresistible drive to find out how far equine therapy could take me. I couldn't get enough of this new feeling of calm and assurance—something that Buck Brannaman promises the viewer in *Buck*.

Reflections: The Power of Wonder

When my circumstances brought me to my knees and I felt like I would never rise up again, I was given the gift of a horse story. *God* knew I could be led back to myself through the relationship I would have with horses. If you are in the same position there is no accident or wonder that you picked up my book.

There are very simple and inexpensive things you can do to get started on the revival of your life. Go to the library and borrow a film about horses, or take a drive to a local ranch or horse rescue facility. The peace, connection, and pathways to healing that came from my time with horses—in equine therapy, volunteering, and caring for them—has been and continues to be profound. I always leave with a feeling of accomplishment and intimacy. It is amazing that some of the most abused horses, like my friend Monty, will allow me to lead him and feed him. He knows that I have gone through my trials as well and when I'm around him and my other horse friends they always greet me with curiosity, humor, and attention. They need my help to take care of them and my soul needs them too. There is nothing quite like a relationship with a horse.

Seek out volunteer opportunities with nonprofits that take care of, and showcase, equine centers. I promise their transformative nature will blow you away.

CHAPTER 4

PRESSING IN

A good rider can hear his horse speak to him.
A great rider can hear his horse whisper.
—Author unknown

The drive out to the Wonder Equine Therapy Center is a long one but the time it takes to get there is a therapy all by itself. The drive is calming and sets the tone for the equine therapy experience. There is nothing like the scent and scenery while driving through the redwoods, past open hillsides and lakes.

When I arrived at my destination, I saw Dr. Lambert in the middle of the pasture walking with her horses. She saw me pull alongside the fence to park and walked toward me to greet me. The drive there was surreal enough but the experience at her center was beyond anything I could have imagined. This was not my first experience working with her and the horses, but this time, a door to all that kept me trapped was opened up and I have never been the same since.

I had been to the equine therapy center once before when I initially met Dr. Lambert. This session would be a very different one.

I had been seeing Dr. Lambert for some time and had done a lot of one-on-one work with her in her office. When I had an appointment with the horses it felt like a fresh new learning experience. It was often unpredictable, intimate, and fun. I never knew how the horses would react to me but there was a lightness to my experience with them. Every equine session was different and every facilitator or therapist had a different way of having the horses work with me. On this visit I sat with Dr. Lambert in plastic chairs placed in the middle of a riding ring, with all four horses milling around us.

We started our session that day talking about what I had been experiencing recently, just as we did when I went to see her for my regular appointments in her office. I wasn't paying much attention to the horses as I was engaged in our conversation. One of her horses, named Wonder, has a very inquisitive and naughty personality. He always led the herd and as he came closer to Dr. Lambert, the others followed him and gathered around us. I was interrupted mid-sentence by the huge head of a horse.

May is a mare and she seemed to want to get in on our conversation in some way, standing so close to me she was touching my shoulder. May didn't want to be on the outside listening in, and appeared to have something to say. She moved right between Dr. Lambert and me, cutting us off from each other, almost saying to us, Okay let's get started!

The other horses had entered our small circle and when I looked around to see all these horses engaged in our conversation, I realized that my communication with Dr. Lambert wasn't foreign to them; it was as if they understood what I was saying and wanted to help.

We finished talking and put the horses out to pasture so that Dr. Lambert could create four squares of plastic pipe in the ring. The squares were large enough for me and one horse to walk in and stand comfortably. I call this the therapy of "pressing in." In my session I named three feelings or subjects that held the most emotional charge for me. I gave a name to each of these feelings

and assigned them to a square. I named my squares *abandonment,*
fear, and *grief.*

Many months passed since my first encounter with the horses
and I had done a lot of healing. So much that I created the square
of *reunion with my son.*

May and I had the most intimate rapport, so she was going to
help me in this session. I took her by the lead rope and headed to the
square called abandonment. She hesitated a bit but as I talked to her
she came in right behind me. Abandonment was an uncomfortable,
but very familiar subject to me. It didn't have the emotional charge
it once had in my life. As I stood next to May, she stood still. She
was like a horse statue, looking straight ahead. I whispered to her,
"What do I need to know about abandonment now?" It was the
first conversation I had with a horse, and the reply was in the form
of thoughts. I knew I wasn't making up a desired answer because
I could not have replied with the insight this answer had. She said
to me, *This is an old story, the one with baby Charla. It is no longer the truth*
with grownup Charla. This story has been told, you can release it now; you can
just let it go.

I was shocked! I was adopted and for most of my life abandonment
had shaped my identity. I had seen being adopted in a negative way
as it was portrayed that way. This made me very independent and
self-reliant. It also shaped the part of my personality that made me
isolate when I didn't feel I was good enough. The reality was that
my adoption was the best decision that my birth mother made for
me. I could let go of the negative connotations now because they
were no longer applicable. I may have had disconnected feelings
in relationships, especially with my family members—with the
exception of my Dad—but that was over now and it was time to
release it in the square of abandonment. When I felt and heard
May's message it was as if I was listening to a trusted advisor that
had wisdom and love for me.

The next square we entered was the square of fear. Because the
word carried so much charge for me—it was an emotional boulder

in my life—May resisted walking into it. As I stood with her outside the square of fear I noticed her resistance and when we got close enough to cross over the plastic pipe she stopped completely. I have always had the presence of fear in my life and that in itself isn't necessarily harmful. But after years of defending myself in court cases and being tied up in litigation that took its toll on me in so many ways, I was always fearful of what would happen next.

During this new type of therapy with the horses, I was aware of how present I was in the moment. It was imperative because of the risk involved that could result in serious injury. Anything could happen at any moment to scare the horses, such as a backfire from a car or a wild animal that ran into their space at the ranch. I have even seen a horse get spooked and rear up for no apparent reason. Dr. Lambert had warned me about this and she went to great lengths to teach me how to lead them and hold their rope. Every precaution was teaching me a new way to be aware in life and how to take care of me.   Being aware was good; hypervigilance was not. Dr. Lambert told me that the horses would do what they had to do to protect themselves in an emergency and this hit home. I learned that it was natural and normal for them to react and run in the face of danger; in fact, it is crucial to their survival. I saw that my behavior mimicked theirs when I left my home in Southern California, and my son, in order to save myself from more harm. This example allowed me to release the guilt I was carrying over my decision to leave.

This realization was so foreign to me. Why didn't all the doctors present this information in this way? Why didn't I hear this from the many therapists or groups I attended? I had spent so much of the past years disassociating from the pain and fear, but now, in order to bring my therapy horse into a square, I had to be present, open to and observant of her feelings so she could understand how to navigate mine. Trusting myself to do this with her made my fears vanish. And trusting anything, much less a horse, seemed completely counterintuitive. But May sensed my change and she stepped into the square with me.

I knew that having experienced so much trauma, I displayed symptoms of post-traumatic stress disorder. Standing with May in the square of fear helped me to understand that I could learn to manage fear and hypervigilance with patience, self-care routines, and practice. One day it wouldn't have to be the way I responded to life. I had gotten a glimpse of what I felt like being calm in a small square with a large animal and not having irrational fear. I didn't know if I could ever be free from my memories, but I did see that I was much better in the moment and this allowed me to feel freer about the past and relax a bit more. This feeling of calm was astounding for me.

I stood in the square of fear and knew that I had experienced a profound change with fear and its ability to sweep me away. I leaned against May and I tuned into her thoughts about me and fear. *I know all about fear,* she said, *but you are not fearful.* She said I had become fearless and that's how she relates to me. When I let her message in, I was standing there, fearless! I felt that way and my neurosystem agreed. I was calm and strong in my stance and maybe even a bit taller. In that square I experienced being fearless and fear no longer had the same power over me.

I turned to see where the other horses were in the pasture and they were at least one hundred yards away from us. One of them got spooked and bucked and ran from the herd. After a short period of time he calmed down and came back to the herd and his irritation from the incident subsided. The horses grazed, ran, and played with each other. They didn't take their emotions and make things worse. I never observed their fear or irritation with each other to be a permanent state of being. From watching them I understood a healthy way to feel my fears, react, and then let them go.

My new understanding allows me to notice my fears and choose to react for a shorter period of time but not allow the emotion to take me out, all the while staying present and safe. I rarely allow the feeling of fear to grow into a state of hypervigilance like it used to. I am cautious in what I choose to look at and read. I don't usually get sucked into stories about violence. I am aware of my surroundings and what is going on in the world but I choose not to get pulled into the fear-filled stories. I feed my mind with positive and thought-provoking subjects that interest me and help me to grow as a woman who wants to be a part of positive change. I love meeting and learning about people who are committed to doing the same. These actions allow me to live a peaceful life knowing that when a negative emotion comes, I have the knowledge and the experience to handle it and not let it take me over.

What happened in the square of grief changed everything for me. This emotion directly tied to the loss of my son consumed my physical and psychological self in a way I never thought possible. Even if I felt the onset of grief I became overwhelmed because my experience with this emotion was all consuming. This was the third square to enter and it was the hottest part of the afternoon. I remember leading May over to that square but her walk had slowed, her hoofs were kicking up the dirt, and dust was flying all around us. May's willingness to enter the other squares had been easy compared to this square—it held the deepest challenge and sorrow for me and she could tell.

Forcing a quarter horse into a place I had so much trepidation about would be impossible. Who in her right mind would want to do that? May mirrored my dread about grief, the one emotion I had no idea what to do with or how to handle when it came on. It was triggered by the natural grieving for my son and the unending longing for him. That sadness was the leading edge of the wave. It picked up more power and strength as I continued to think about him, and my connection to him. Memories of him as a little boy and our life together inevitably turned to thoughts of loss. This also led to unanswered questions of where and how he was and what he must be thinking about me. When I replayed my decision to quit fighting and leave him, grief became a huge wave crashing down on top of me and scrambling my mind in the undercurrent of survival.

I remembered the emotions turning into physical pain in my chest and heart. The grief was mixed with many other feelings and as I continue to heal, I have learned that one of those was the warm wash of shame. All of this mental torture was part of a mother's natural longing for her child, her son, her love. I was lucky if I could keep myself present in any way when the wave of grief and shame came. Most of the time it was like being washed out to sea after being lifted up and then pounded down by it. The emotion would subside and I felt myself calm down, breathe normally again, and be so exhausted that it took days to recover from this upheaval.

I knew I had to change my response to grief but up to this point I had learned very little about how to grieve my missing son. I was here to learn what I hoped would heal my heart and allow me to continue to move forward with my life. I had no idea if grief could ever be gone from my heart but I had to learn how to manage it.

I stood next to May in front of the plastic pipe lying in the dirt. I couldn't prod her into the square. She was immovable; she wasn't going in. There was some part of me that constantly lived in a state of grief. I didn't realize this before, but I needed her help to release me in every way.

After several more attempts to get May in the square she lifted one hoof then another, moving very slowly until she stood in the square. Then she stood motionless, barely breathing. As we stood together she turned and looked at me as if to say, *I want you to know what it's like to feel safe, solid, and secure. Not tossed about by this wave of your emotion.* We stood still together, my hands on her neck, petting her and thanking her for coming in with me.

I was scared. But there I stood trusting this twelve-hundred-pound animal, open, raw, vulnerable, and so small in every way.

I stood on the right side of May's body and stroked her back and belly. The sun beat down on us and everything was silent. As I stroked her she transmitted instructions to me. She asked me to lean on her and against her and put my arms over her back. I trusted she wouldn't run off while my whole body lay on hers.

As I did this she communicated with me in a way I would understand. I've experienced being in the ocean and felt the ebb and the flow of the waves. I knew the sensation of being tossed around knowing I wasn't in control, but in time I learned to navigate the waves. I learned this when I took up surfing as a girl growing up and playing at the beach. This was a language with sensation that I could understand. I continued to press into her side I felt her say, *When you feel the wave of sadness and despair approaching, do what you think you cannot do—lean into it. Come on, try it with me here. I won't move. It will be safe for you. I will teach you how to navigate this and you will be okay.*

My mind raced with doubts about what I was hearing from her and I discounted the communication I was receiving. I thought, *She can hurt you. Don't surrender to this. You won't be safe. This isn't something you know for sure.* And on and on it went. But I had no more room for doubt. I wasn't trying this form of therapy to fail. In fact, there was no more room in my life to fail. From this point on I had to trust.

It was important to associate with memories of overcoming challenges in my life so I could tackle the biggest challenge so far. As I leaned into May, she told me she would be the wave of grief. As overwhelmed as I had been with this monster, I was leaning into it by leaning into her. Minutes passed and as they did I was aware of my breathing and thoughts as they slowed down and I began to relax. I steadied myself in that moment and imagined myself relaxing into this force of grief.

The next transmission came from May. *You're in the ocean of emotion and as you press into me you feel the swell of a large wave come upon you. Do what you have to do when you're in the ocean. Calculate when you need to take a breath of air and as the wave is ready to pound you, dive under it.* Then May said, *Duck under my neck like you would the wave. Trust that you will come up on the other side of my neck and of the wave. Grief and I are the same wave; we can both kill you.* I was scared to duck under her neck. What if she spooked and ran over me while I was in such a vulnerable position? But I had to trust her. I had to take a breath, dive under the wave, and hold my breath until the wave rolled over me.

As I moved toward her head and ducked under her neck she said to me, *You have enough energy and strength to come back up. Now roll under my neck and move to my other side.* After I did that it was as if I had come up for air after a wave had just passed. I felt relieved. The power of this horse and the power of the waves in the ocean were the same: I had dodged getting smashed by that power and I was in the calm between the sets. I had made it to May's other side and she was steadfast, strong, and understood my fear. The next thought from May was, *Press into the wave called grief; it won't be against you. It will support you, like I am supporting you now. You are as vulnerable with me as you are with the emotion, but you are strong enough to maneuver the power of it. Now you know what to do.*

As I stood there in the square I released my fear of it. May's willingness had transformed my greatest burden, one I had carried for years. The equine therapy sessions were all critical for me and I healed by leaps and bounds when I worked with the horses.

I wanted to test my ability to manifest my heart's desire—a reunion with my son. As I tugged on May's lead rope to enter the last square, reunion with my son, I noticed the other horses a couple hundred yards away, grazing. They were consumed in what they were doing as we entered the square. This square felt new, fresh, and open to possibility. It was a place of the future; nothing of the past was there. It was effortless to lead May into this square and she seemed to know we were almost finished.

I spoke with her now like I would with an intimate friend. I told her about my son and how we were separated, how much I would love to see him and fantasized about meeting him. I told her that he could trust me in this new time and place and we could start anew. May looked right at me, listening intently. I glanced up and saw the other four horses galloping toward us as if they had overheard my conversation and wanted to be part of it. They ran up to the fence as close to us as they could get, startling Dr. Lambert and me. The horses wanted to share in this future celebration, I thought. They wanted to see my son with me, in a square of love, safety, and happiness.

For several months following the session I didn't get to see May, but when I finally returned she remembered me. I had nothing but adoration and love for her and I showered her with those feelings every time I was with her. I had gone through many positive changes in my life and she sensed all of them. But I still had not seen or talked with my son for many years due to the forced separation also known as parental alienation.

I continued with many avenues of therapeutic work to heal my heart, and was visited by dreams of the possibility of a reunion. This brought me strength and when I thought about my son it wasn't as painful anymore, and the longing that had previously filled my mind was not so overwhelming. I had more freedom to think in positive ways when I thought of him and us, and my curiosity about him didn't have the negative charge it once had.

Reflections: Pressing In

I learned how to press into the most painful places in my story with the help of Dr. Lambert and May, the horse. Grief overwhelmed me with all its messy components of pain, fear, and the recurrence of memories of the loss of my son. I believe that these emotions aren't something one must manage but something that we as survivors must learn to let go of and quit managing.

I felt *God's love* for me in that square with May. I know that this same *God* doesn't want me or you to suffer anymore. There are steps to take before the letting go of your story and you start to feel free of the pressure to manage something that has diminished or even destroyed you.

Write down five people who have been supportive of you. Next, write down how they supported you and how you felt in their company. Now use this information to build a support team that can help you untangle the heaviest part of your story, and commit to being supported in the process. If possible, seek counseling from the list you've compiled. Seek an equine therapist or an equine therapy workshop. Be open to all the possibilities of support you're seeking and be on the lookout for the signs that will lead you where you need to go.

I learned to take my deepest grief and turn it into one of greatest victories of all time, while being supported by a thousand-pound horse. Learning to trust and stay present in this lesson has been one of my greatest tests and accomplishments. I trust when you're ready that support will be right outside your door. Believe, just believe.

CHAPTER 5

NEVER GIVE UP MOM

No one else will ever know the strength of my love for you.
After all, you're the only one who knows the sound
of my heart from the inside.
—Kristen Proby, *Fight with Me*

Finding a new way to communicate with my son became my obsession. I wanted him to know I was still alive and thinking of him. I needed him to know I hadn't given up on him or abandoned him. Like any parent, I wanted to share my life, my voice, and my heart with my child; I couldn't give up on my relationship with my son. A force was driving me to find new ways to communicate. Many of these ideas were foreign to me. As I became more grounded in my new apartment, and as my path became clearer and I continued to gain self-confidence, I started to trust my intuition and where I was being led. One night as I was in a light sleep, I heard my son's voice. It was as clear as a bell. I also felt his presence. He said, *Don't give up, Mom.* I knew his voice as well as I knew my own. It was my son!

At this time I was getting ready to accept a position with a new company near my apartment. For the first time in many years

I was completely on my own and though the transition had been a difficult one, I was ready to take the reins of my life again. I was ready to be in a silent environment and trust the voice that comes to me in the silence. I wanted to hear God's opinion. I wanted enough quiet so I would no longer cheat myself out of hearing the *Divine* instructions that would assist me in making a great life for myself. I wanted the impossible to happen; I wanted to hear from my son. I didn't want to rent a room any longer or share a home with another. I needed a whole space for me and what remained of my belongings. I didn't care if this tiny apartment was to be a storage space for a while. I knew I would decorate my storage space and it would be the damn best-looking storage anyone had ever seen.

This was the first time in over two decades that I was living without a title—daughter, wife, mother. Looking back, I would give myself the title of *heroine*, healer of my life. I had been on this therapeutic path for a couple of years, including time with my equine therapist. I didn't go out to be with the horses every week, but I kept my standing appointment with her without fail. Dr. Lambert was the human facilitator in the vast portion of my healing work and I trusted her intuition about me implicitly. Her weekly support was key in rebuilding a life that was strong and positive and stable.

For the first time in years I felt I was okay with just me and what I had in the moment. I had begun to trust the process of life and I felt happy about what I had accomplished. I was open to new possibilities in my life again, as a woman, and I became surer of being in the world again. This was the beginning of embodying being the leading lady in my life, and as I got settled in my new little apartment I continued to calm down. Every time I took a breath I exhaled far longer than the breath I took in. It was as if I had been holding my breath for years and now I was safe enough to exhale. Every time I did the burdens of my past dissipated. In this new space my mind woke up. The silence drew in new dreams and bigger goals, not just hopes. I felt I had what it took to manifest a life of my choosing and out of that grew more strength and the conviction to find a way to my son.

I reached out to friends who had been an important part of my life until my path diverged and I lost track of them. One such friend was a woman named Cristal. We had been very close for several years and when my personal crash came she also had a difficult life transition to go through. I thought of her often and she would appear to me in dreams. Dreams usually prompted a shift in reality. I was ready to have my world grow and this meant having a close friendship with a girlfriend who knew my story. I found her phone number one day and called it hoping it was still the right one. It was!

This started the kind of friendship I desired and it was the same for her. We spent many evenings talking about our past and discussing the difficulties of my present separation from my son and what could be done to change it. There were still so many days and nights when the longing to hear his voice, to know how he was, where he was, or see his face, was almost too much to bear. I had come a long way in reestablishing myself and I knew I couldn't allow my grief and sadness to take hold of me and drag me backward. This was an emotional edge I knew all about and being too close to it or reminiscing about the past for too long was dangerous for me.

I still had anger about this injustice along with hopeless feelings, but this time I used these feelings to support me, just like grief did in the riding ring with May. I didn't allow them to swamp me and sweep me away emotionally. I got on the other side of them by pressing into them. It was uncomfortable and sad but I was learning to be the master of these emotions and I knew I was getting better at it. I had come to accept that there was no cure for my broken heart, but I was healing from these circumstances, and still there was this horrible separation from my son. I knew there was something more I could do; I just didn't know what.

One night, as my girlfriend and I were talking—something that was life-giving for me—our conversation touched me and held me like a mother holds a child. It gave me a kind of comfort that I had not felt in a long time and for the first time I understood what the word *cherished* meant. I know we felt the same way about each other and this was food for my heart and soul. I was growing in my life like a seed that had been buried under the snow and was now pushing up through the soil to become what it was always meant to be.

Cristal suggested creating a blog to share my thoughts and feelings for my son. This was a phenomenal idea with a couple of glaring exceptions. First, I had no idea how to create one, and I had always felt inferior to the complexity of computers. Second, my typing skills were lacking. However, my biggest concern was that I was afraid to go public about my situation with my son.

I had needed my anonymity to feel safe and the privacy it gave me also created the space to heal from the trauma and dream about having a future again. I didn't want to destroy that; there was nothing more sacred for me than feeling safe in my world and the peace that it brought.

We discussed the idea further and I started to envision it as a bridge of words written with love to my son. This vision of a bridge reminded me of when I had tied the dried yellow rose to the Golden Gate Bridge a couple of years before and the promise I made to myself then to continue on, and not give up on myself, no matter how difficult. This time my promise would include my son, and the next bridge I would cross would be one toward him.

There were so many years I spent in silence, where I felt I had no voice, but everything has an ending and now it was time for my silence to end. I knew going public and reaching out to my son had its dangers, so I prayed for guidance with what to say to him, and how to create a world of words that would allow me the freedom to express how I felt about him. I wanted clear guidelines on what I should and should not write about. I didn't want to reignite the circumstances of the past and talk about the abuses, injustices, and the hardships. I wanted to use the anger I still had as an incentive to make my next steps positive and feed the burning desire to find my purpose. At this point I knew I didn't want my words to be filled with bitterness.

This was a new beginning for me and a brand new way to use my voice and share it with him. I saw it as God giving me safe passage to love him and myself, and to no longer suffer the silence as his mother.

When this opportunity to write was presented to me, the "what ifs" dominated my thoughts. What if he never saw my blog? What if he saw it and didn't want to read it? But without the risk of writing to my absent son I knew all he had was an invisible mother. Without writing to him I would surely leave a legacy of mystery and pain for him. After praying and asking for the clear guidelines on what to write, I was given *Divine* guidance. *Write about your Love for him.*

At first this thought seemed limited. But now, after writing to him for the past four years, I understand that this *blog of love* wasn't just for him, but for many others who knew this type of loss. It became a portal for the years that had been denied him. I had the bulk of the pictures from his birth to age eleven, so I used them to create an online family album. One more piece of the bridge was built.

Once I confirmed that this could be a safe way to communicate and give him back his history as a child, I knew it was the right thing to do. My girlfriend Cristal was a techie so she found the best way to construct the blog and showed me how to use it.

This was the first time since leaving all the court battles behind that I would speak out and have a voice. The distance and time I gave myself was essential in growing stronger in mind and body. I had to formulate a purer voice and steadiness in my soul. I knew the harmful oppression of being silenced had to come to an end. *Without a vision the people will perish* (Proverbs 29:18), and without a voice I believe they will too.

I wrestled with the title of the most important project of my life. We laughed about some of the suggested titles and others were two thumbs down. One night as I was getting ready for bed I remembered what my son had said to me in a dream. *Don't give up*

Mom. I took his words of inspiration and decided to name my blog *Never Give Up Mom.*

It was so striking to me, and it came from him as well as my decision to not give up. This was the first sentence that uncaged my voice. It felt like a command and an affirmation. It became my mantra of hope as well as the title of my blog. This bridge of love and support to my son was under construction and all I had to do was write and press "Publish."

This avenue of expression has been one of the most important things I have done to take my power back. It also gave me a tangible way to express myself to him. I wanted to be his mother, and this was the first physical expression of that.

I didn't really know who would read it, or how the social media world worked, but as I continued to write year after year and gain popularity on Google, our pictures began to merge magically. One night I was playing around on the computer and dared to search for images with my son's name. Wow! A page came up and many of the pictures I had in our family album were in the first third of this page! As I scrolled down the page there were pictures of me next to pictures of him as a baby and his birthdays. All merged together forever. I could never have figured out how to do that myself, but the *Divine* (and Google) put them together beautifully! It was one of the most elevated moments of my life. We did it! My girlfriend, God, and Google. I knew if my son googled himself he would find my blog and know that I hadn't given up on him or forgotten him.

I no longer had to fear that he would never know what was in my heart. I didn't have the same fear that he would have the mystery and pain that surrounded my disappearance and so-called abandonment of him. This was very important to me as I remembered the pain I had in my childhood about being given up for adoption. I went to great lengths to find my birth parents and work through the feelings of abandonment and hurt. I remember when I met them what a relief it was to be able to make sense of those missing pieces of my life. *Never Give Up Mom* became the evidence that I had not abandoned him and that I would not, and could not, ever truly leave him. What my blog did for me was crucial; it gave me an avenue to explore, express, and share my *voice* with him.

The day came that *Never Give Up Mom* was live and I stepped way outside my comfort zone to write and publish my first post and allow my thoughts, my voice, and my heart to be heard around the world. Emotionally it was daunting, and it was crystal clear I had fear in doing this. But in every step I took to reclaim a life worth living, I received more personal power. Out of the silence I grew a new voice—the voice of a mother's love that is unending and unconditional. With this confidence I felt the power to continue in the face of anything that could test me and try to stop me from writing my blog. This power was the motivation I needed to get past the difficulty of writing the first post, then another. Each time I finished a post and published it, the risk became smaller and the potential reward of a reunion became greater. I approached my doubts about writing by telling myself that almost everyone knows how to write, and this basic skill that I had surely would lend itself to the worthiest of causes. I used to be a writer for my school paper, therefore I had enough credentials to author this blog! Of course I had doubts about being a writer, but my heart was screaming to be heard and I had become strong enough to open myself up in such a public way.

My girlfriend supported me and coached me through the first post. I remember spending so much time poring over every detail. And I remember praying about what I should and shouldn't write and asking for clear answers and guidelines. My prayer was answered through a feeling I received and I experienced a calm certainty about what to do. The guidelines to write were these: *Write from your heart. Tell your son the stories of your life, keeping things general. Don't be afraid to share your sadness about being separated from him. What is most important is to tell him about your love for him and the hope you have in reuniting with him someday.* I would follow these guidelines and within these boundaries a bridge would be built.

Never Give Up Mom's first post was written on November 12, 2012.

I AM A NEVER GIVE UP MOM … Hello world!

Welcome to my first attempt at blogging, and a message to all moms and dads who will NEVER GIVE UP…

I hope that you will come back often as I begin my journey of expression on this very important project.

My first post was the biggest step I had taken to make a connection to my son with the fewest words. It has now been four years since that first post and I been contacted by other parents who share the same sadness and hopelessness, and have been told not to give up writing.

Never Give Up Mom has been a catalyst for healing the separation, and has been, at times, a place I could express my outrage about my experience with parental alienation. I learned that righteous anger is healthy in that it gives a person a strong reason to live and as long as I continued to write within the guidelines I was given, my righteous anger propelled me to keep writing.

There have been many months in which I experienced great trepidation writing a post, and other times I looked forward to expressing my feelings and stories, placing one more piece on this bridge of hope. With every passing month I wrote, I became stronger in my resolve to one day reunite with my son. Every time I received a comment, positive or negative—and I am thankful there were few negative comments—that feedback became the wind that carried me to the next month.

I had no sign that my son might be reading the blog until one day I checked the comment section and saw someone had left a comment with his name on it! It was May 23 at 4:00 a.m. and I stared at the comment for an hour, reading it over and again.

Reflections: Never Give Up Mom

Never Give Up Mom became my mantra and personal promise. In opening myself to this opportunity and stepping through that door I found the support I needed to get through that challenging time. I also found out that the friend who was the engineer of my blog had been denied a life with her mother when she was young. This gave both of us the opportunity to heal our wounds and wounds of many others. I continue to have appointments with the *Divine* and to build a bridge of communication to my son through my blog.

Through the commitment to never give up and the willingness to write about my love, I co-created a new world for myself. What would you start in your life that would be of benefit to you? How would your example of following through benefit others?

I've grown stronger and more aware of some of my readers who are victims of parent alienation or abduction, or for other reasons have lost years with someone they love. *Never Give Up Mom* is now in its fifth year with more than seven thousand views and three thousand visitors from around the globe.

CHAPTER 6

LANGUAGE OF THE HEART

A horse will cross any bridge you build, as long as the first
one is from him to you.
—Author unknown

I've never let up in my search to find new ways to connect with my son. In one of my trips to the local library I found a movie titled *You Can Heal Your Life* by author and visionary, Louise Hay. The film is about a woman on her journey of healing and like myself, she was in the midst of change and deep personal transformation.

I ended up renting this film and its companion DVD with interviews of Hay House authors and viewing them dozens of times. The film was the first thing I turned on in the morning while getting ready for work, and often I would sit by the fire in the evening and watch the interviews with Wayne Dyer, Louise Hay, and an unknown author to me, Gregg Braden. Every time I put the DVD in and heard the opening music, I felt as if I was receiving more clues to my unfolding journey. It was the sustenance that fed my heart and soul. I couldn't afford cable television, so the library was my resource for information, inspiration, and entertainment.

After viewing the movie one morning I realized that I didn't just hope to connect with my son—I *needed* to. In one of the interviews on the companion DVD, author, visionary, and scientist Gregg Braden discusses an experiment that involved dividing a particle of matter. The experiment was taken from a field of science known as Quantum Entanglement. It was conducted in Geneva, Switzerland in 1997, the same year my son was born. The scientist took a particle of matter and split it in two. The pieces were then separated by fourteen miles. When one of those pieces was disturbed, the other piece, miles away, showed distress. Braden went on to say that one of the pieces of matter showed signs of distress even before the other particle was disturbed. This newfound information of our inseparable nature was the next *Divine* appointment, suggesting that my son and I were still connected, and the messages, dreams, and whispers of thoughts I was receiving were indeed from him.

I had been inviting my son to connect with me by my thoughts but what I learned was that our hearts are the strongest electric and magnetic field in our bodies. With this information my heart mended even more. This was and always has been the heart of the matter for me—to know that the feeling of being connected to him isn't just wishful thinking. It's fact, and I can trust the different ways we were communicating with each other. Gregg Braden's interview was not just informative but transformational for me.

I had experienced this kind of separation and reunion myself. When I was thirty-one years of age I decided to try to find my birth parents. The impetus for this search was the news that my best girlfriend was going to have to abort her baby in her second trimester after finding out that if born, the baby would not survive. This news was so sobering it prompted me to begin my search so I could find out what my DNA was.

I sought out a Los Angeles County Department of Public Social Services social worker after many winding roads of leads and information. I hoped my appointment with this man would lead me to find my birth parents. I found out that the county had my adoption records and by law were not going to give them to me. I went anyway to see if I could extract any further information about my background and my birth parents. I was so nervous driving to the appointment that I had a slight accident when I got too close to the curb with my car. The possibility of discovering what was kept from me all my life was exciting and nerve-racking, but once the path was opened for me to find out about my origins, I was driven to know. I believed it was my God-given right to know, just as it is my son's to know about me.

After spending an hour with the social worker asking questions and trying to get more information from him, he explained that by law he could not give me my paperwork, but what he would tell me for a fact was that more often than not *when one member of the triad (the birth family) started to search for the other members, the other members began to seek each other out as well*. I found this news fascinating and wondered if that would happen with me. I'd known all my life that I'd been born to different parents than the ones that raised me and my desire to find my birth parents wasn't simply because I wanted to know about my DNA and my biological family. There was a force so powerful to reunite with them that I couldn't fully comprehend or explain it … then.

The social worker turned out to be right. My search prompted my birth father to look for my birth mother, as they had parted before my birth. After a two-year search I was given my birth father's phone number by a woman who helped me find him. I met my birth father for the first time since the day he signed the papers for my adoption. We talked on the phone for hours and the emotion that came out of his side of our conversation was beautiful. The secret veil was lifted.

He told me he had started to search for my birth mother about one year before I found him, which was about one year after I began my search. He talked about the feelings that prompted him to find her and make amends. After his initial contact he continued to stay in touch periodically to say hello. We were all linked energetically and just as the social worker had told me about family members beginning a search around the same time, this was an example of quantum entanglement. After the initial phone conversation with my birth father, he contacted my birth mother and told her I had found him and would like to have a conversation with her. Within an hour after I hung up the phone with him, I received a call from her.

It's been decades since my initial desire to meet my birth parents had been satisfied, and this led me to heal the feelings of abandonment and the unanswered questions I had. It's been an interesting experience to meet and see who I look like, laugh like, and where some of my characteristics come from. Living with the label of adoption often shaped my world in a negative way, and I wanted my son to know the truth about where I went and why I couldn't be with him now. I was not going to carry the burdens of past shame and guilt into my present relationship with my son.

Since watching Gregg Braden's interview in *You Can Heal Your Life* and reading several articles on his beliefs about connection, I could identify my emotional pulls and longings when I was a child and now I understood the science of connection that had always been there with my birth parents. I grew up wondering why I experienced unrest. It was a feeling of wanting to be connected and I knew that my feeling wouldn't go away or unnoticed. My desire to know them was just like the particle that was split and placed fourteen miles apart. I had experienced this separation myself and understood its origins of longing for reconnection. I had explored the subject with my birth parents, and now was continuing that exploration with the separation of my son. I'd been given the gift of this information and I believed it. I would find a different way to connect and reunite with my son. To some Gregg Braden's information may have sounded outlandish but for me it was indisputable.

I reviewed his interview so many times that with every post I wrote and every prayer I spoke my intention became clearer and my energy stronger. This is the *Divine's* example of connection in its highest form. What I prayed for was safe, open, and loving communication. This was the way to tell my son all that I had wanted to say to him, and this form of communing with my son was pure and healing for my soul. My writing reached out to him and started the reunification process. I now had a place where my heart could be heard and I learned to develop the *language of my heart.*

I continued to study Gregg Braden's ideas, experiments, and beliefs about healing and connection. I noted the following ideas from his book, *The Divine Matrix: Bridging Time, Space, Miracles, and Belief,* and from interviews he had given. He put into words what I have felt as truth all along. These are some of my favorite quotes that have helped me continue to build my faith.

"When we form heart-centered beliefs within our bodies, in the language of physics we're creating the electrical and magnetic expression of them as waves of energy, which aren't confined to our hearts or limited by the physical barrier of our skin and bones. So clearly we're speaking to the world around us in each moment of every day through a language that has no words: the belief-waves of our hearts."

"We are never more than a belief away from our deepest love, deepest healing, and most profound miracles."

"All it takes is one person in any generation to heal a family's limiting beliefs."

"Both science and mysticism describe a force that connects everything together and gives us the power to influence how matter behaves—and reality itself— simply through the way we perceive the world around us."

"Through the power of our forgotten inner technology, we can heal, bilocate, be everywhere at once, remote-view, connect telepathically, choose peace, and do everything in between."

"Even though we may be physically separated from one another, we can still be in instantaneous communication"

In my relentless desire to formulate the language of my heart I recalled occasions with the horses that at the time had seemed so bizarre and random. I continued to connect the dots between the power and language of the heart and it made sense why the horses had acted the way they did. On one of my first appointments with Dr. Lambert at the equine center, I was telling the story of what led me to leave my son and move to Northern California. I didn't immediately notice the horses and their reactions, but Dr. Lambert did. I watched her eyes as she turned away from me to look in their direction. Even though I had just been introduced to this herd of horses—and they were at the far end of the pasture—they felt the rawness of my emotions. One of the horses went up on his hind legs, growling and clawing at one of the other horses. They all seemed agitated and bolted out of the corner of the pasture. In that instance I witnessed just how powerful my emotional language was for them. I was speaking very slowly and quietly but I no longer wanted to hide and control the rage I felt inside.

I knew I had come far in healing my grief and losses, but there was something else gnawing inside me. The word forgiveness began showing up in conversations with others. Its frequency was enough to let me know this might be related to the feeling inside of me. I vividly remember a casual conversation with a work acquaintance when out of the blue she said to me, "You might consider the idea of forgiving everyone in your past, including your ex-husband." I hardly knew her at the time, but I remember noticing that she always appeared happy and genuine. She had been watching me and my journey and she obviously knew something about forgiveness that I didn't understand. I looked at her with the word *crazy* in my mind.

I gave this concept of forgiveness some time and in all honesty I figured I couldn't do it, even if there was a slight chance that I wanted to. I also knew I had the burden from an unforgiving heart and with this I couldn't be completely free. I wanted to keep going and get beyond my past and I knew this was key for my growth. I stayed attentive to the concept of forgiveness and how it was affecting me. Each time I was with the horses I observed their nature and how they treated each other when one got upset. They didn't hold grudges or have an unforgiving nature and when one horse had a problem with another it might give a little kick or bite or try to run the other horse off, but it was over quickly. Then they went back to roam, graze, and play. They had a hierarchy in the herd but the alpha male or female never oppressed the rest of the herd. The freedom in their hierarchy had few rules but the ones they did have were known among them for the good of all.

It wasn't until years later that I discovered what made sense about forgiveness and why it was so damn hard to forgive with the explanation I was raised with. Forgiving my ex-husband and all the people who were involved with the loss of my son felt disjointed for me, not true, and just plain BS. The concept that I grew up with was always to forgive or reconcile with the other person, to turn the other cheek, but in my case that was simply not possible. I learned that forgiveness wasn't an intellectual process and by forgiving my ex-husband for my son's abduction and parental alienation, or the bank for the fraudulent foreclosure, I would be looking at forgiveness in the wrong manner, because *forgiveness is not finding resolution with the predator.*

Dr. Mario Martinez, a clinical neuropsychologist who studied and taught forgiveness, says this about it, in his book *The MindBody Code*: *"Forgiveness is an act of love to liberate yourself from an enslavement. [...] In the liberation is where the forgiveness comes."*

This description of forgiveness took hold of me and it finally made sense. Dr. Martinez calls this a biocognition process at the level of the mind and body. He went on to say that having righteous anger is healthy in healing from trauma, and that one didn't have to condone the act or forgive or reconcile with the predator. He goes on to say that in order to change the beliefs that limit your health, longevity and success one needs to see what wounded them. Betrayal, shame and abandonment are the primal wounds that result in a person giving away their power. In my case I experienced all of these throughout the court cases for my son's custody. Now with this new knowledge about the helpful meaning of forgiveness and righteous anger I continue to take back my power.

I continue to deconstruct the barriers I built around my heart because I want to connect on a heart level in my relationships. In fact, I *know* I need to in order to live a happy and healthy life, and with the knowledge and practice of self-empowerment, my writing and general communication becomes clearer and the tone of sorrow continues to fade as a result. Forgiveness is an act of liberation for me; now the language of my heart can be heard more freely and I continue to connect on a deeper level.

Reflections: Language of the Heart

My wish to connect and belong has been a strong desire all my life. Through this experience of separation from my son, I've had a profound urge to have my voice heard. I'm grateful for the internal work I've accomplished and for never giving up on what the true description of connection is. The power I've received in forgiving myself is astonishing. My voice would never have been heard if I hadn't been willing to go through the darkness and misunderstood nature of forgiveness. After forgiving myself and others in turn, letting go of the shame is a natural progression. Ultimately, my voice became softer when speaking about my story.

The world that lives in you wants to reside peacefully and harmoniously. Do what you must to let go of the guilt and shame that isn't yours, and never was. Work toward feeling peaceful, and the voice of your spirit will emerge.

That is one of the most empowering things you will ever experience. This quote by Frederick Buechner embodies just what I mean.

You can kiss your family and friends good-bye and put miles between you, but at the same time you carry them with you in your heart, your mind, your stomach, because you do not just live in a world but a world lives in you. — Frederick Buechner, *Telling the Truth*.

CHAPTER 7

IN FINDING PURPOSE
IN MY PAIN

*Losing someone important makes you reevaluate yourself
and your purpose. Healing the hurt of separation comes,
not by dwelling on what you have lost, but by helping God
revitalize who you are and what you can do.*
—V. Gilbert Beers, *Finding Purpose in Your Pain*

Discovering that I had the power to connect with my son through the language of my heart altered my life and made it possible to reconnect to the nurturing part of being his mother. Finding a description of forgiveness that liberated me while understanding that my anger was righteous and essential to my healing was transformative. I didn't know that using my experience to show *God's love* would ever be something I would do until I received a very important call from a close friend who knew my story about the loss of my son.

I didn't talk with her often, but when I did she intuited details without my having to tell her. Karina and her mother had been a part of every intimate celebration in my life in Northern California.

They were guests at my wedding and an integral part of our lives when my son was born. I knew Karina felt my pain and was careful with her words to me when we spoke. She didn't want me to work harder in our conversation than I already had to because she could hear the strain in my voice even when I thought I was hiding it. There was silence when she listened to me talk about my son and we were both worried for him and wondered where he was. She was caring, kind, and trying to come up with any solutions that might help ease my pain.

She paused in our conversation and I knew she was holding something back. She was a woman who had lived through her own share of heartaches and terror in an unspeakable car accident. She has fought hard and found her way through it all with bravery, dignity, and grace.

I had friends that vanished when I fell apart, but there were some that stayed right by my side and she was one of them. We lived hundreds of miles away from each other and I hadn't seen her in years, so when her call came I was surprised and elated and wanted nothing more than to speak candidly with her. I protected our call as if my life depended on it because I knew she always put a great deal of thought into her words.

This time, she gave me a golden nugget of advice: "Charla, let there be a purpose in your pain." I was startled. I had recently read a book titled *Finding Purpose in Your Pain*, which I had come across while cleaning out a garage and helping friends get ready for their move. Karina, it turned out, hadn't read the book, but she understood the concept well.

This was the next *Divine* appointment with the kind of story that was very similar to mine. The person I was helping swore she had never seen the book and didn't know where it came from. I read the title and quickly looked inside to see what it was about and I asked if I could borrow it. I knew it held significant answers for me.

I interpreted it as a message about what was ahead of me. *Finding Purpose in Your Pain* is a little book with a big message, and it seemed to be written just for me. Once I had the conversation with Karina, I put even more stock in what both the author and my friend said. I paid extra attention to what started to show up and how I would apply the wisdom about purpose and pain. I was ready to receive this spiritual assignment.

According to V. Gilbert Beers, the author of *Finding Purpose in Your Pain*, "whatever pain you are experiencing, you can use it as a blessing to help others." This book helped me have the fortitude to continue on. The mere act of looking for purpose in your pain gives you the power to live from a stronger standpoint. The title of chapter nine is *"SUFFERING, Digging for Thorns as They Go Deeper."* This chapter talks about the sudden loss of a significant person and how it disrupts the flow of your life. It goes on to say that you need to learn how to become a new, different, whole person again despite the loss.

I knew I had to become whole again. I was healing but this was the fifth holiday I had not had any contact with my son, and I felt myself slipping backward toward the edge of a dark abyss. This year was particularly painful so I planned a trip, more like a *walkabout*, to Santa Fe, New Mexico, with my book in hand, to once and for all see if ending my suffering was possible.

This was December 23, 2013, and next to the title I wrote these words: "I am here in Santa Fe, New Mexico. I have suffered long enough." The realization that pain might be inescapable but that suffering isn't, was the moment that I knew I had to end my suffering, no matter how arduous the path.

I went to New Mexico to dig deep and unbeknown to me when I arrived, I would leave without the shame and suffering that coursed through my veins for many years. I wanted to be done with the burden of my story. It was also the moment that I decided there would be purpose in my pain and that my story would go out to others and be a blessing. I didn't have a plan to share my journey with the world, but as time passed the inevitable next step of writing my story became clear.

When I started writing my story it was easy for me to become distracted and be on the move with mundane tasks. Organizing things was a way to cope and to procrastinate. This was my first test of my purpose. I wanted to sit down and start but instead I cleaned closets, refrigerators, and pantries in an obsessive way to avoid facing the difficult memories. I had no experience in writing, especially a story that was *my* story. I thought many times, Who would want to know about a story that is so raw and rough, yet tender?

What kept coming up for me was that everybody has a mother, and so many parents have experienced loss involving their children. The emotional bond that ties parents to their children, and vice versa, is the most fundamental of relationships. So I sat down to begin my writing journey, all the while the voice of doubt continued its diatribe. It said, *Are you crazy to claim this painful part of your past? Are you on a mission for your own demise? You've never written a book before!* On and on the doubts went. To replay my past in order to glean the wisdom of my journey seemed ludicrous, but it became clear this was the next step for me. *Purpose in my pain meant writing this book.* I had to get it down on paper so that my memories no longer had control over me.

I had to excavate my story with utmost care and compassion because not doing so would mean continual pain, and with this pain came diversions and excuses to not continue. I had used many techniques to numb my pain and grief, especially in the early years of the terror and loss. Sorrow acted like a drug that furthered my depression. I experienced a condition called disassociation and saw other women rendered helpless in the grips of it. Yet even with all this human agony, my greatest desire was to keep moving forward.

The next reveal came in New Mexico, while I was in the excavation process. I participated in a support group that was created to uncover the beliefs that we associated most with shame and vulnerability. I was terrified to do this assignment and wondered why I had such resistance. Was I uncovering something so horrific about myself? Was I such a bad daughter, mother, and woman? My fear of uncovering my beliefs about myself gave me valuable insight into how much power they had over me and I knew then that this was the thorn I had to dig out and leave behind.

I sat with the facilitator and one of the participants in a circle. I brought out a box I had painted containing pieces of paper on which I had written seven beliefs and acts I held against myself that I thought were unforgivable. When I brought out each belief or act I had done and read it aloud, it felt like psychic surgery. It didn't seem as if I was exposing such dark secrets, and neither the facilitator nor the witness recoiled in horror. This was a sacred space where we all shared what held the most pain for us. I looked down at the seven pieces of paper laid out on the Indian rug and looked at the thorns that had been part of me, but now the power they held faded right in front of my eyes.

To untangle these beliefs from my core and see them for what they really were in a sacred and safe place, gave me courage to finally let go of the beliefs that were never mine. The stories I told myself as unforgivable were *so wrong* and I knew I'd never have to suffer those false beliefs again. The boulder was rolled away and I was free!

Next I went outdoors and was directed toward a labyrinth. I carried a rock I had painted with bright colors and flowers that looked like they were ready to bloom. The rock symbolized the weight of my past and the flowers the promise of my future. This was a ceremony to honor my whole journey and to place years of misunderstandings, misconceptions, and lies to rest.

With reverence I carried the rock through the labyrinth to its center and placed it down. As I stood there I also acknowledged the depth of my journey. I gave this ceremony my full attention, wrapped the rock in my love, said a silent prayer of gratitude, and turned around slowly to walk back through the maze without the emotional weight I had carried in.

My healing continues to evolve and as it does I know how fortunate I am to have met the teachers and healers that showed me that *compassion is the way,* so that I could be free from my pain. This encouragement led me to believe that the way to proceed wasn't by retelling my story and staying in the past but to continue to grow. Out of growth the right story would reveal itself.

I've learned how to find the strength and courage to continue moving forward and know, with a little faith, the next step of my project will be clear in the right time.

I give credit where it's due to the *Grace* that loves all of us. When I do this I want to feel good and emotionally whole and this allows me to imagine a better future. Every time I choose the positive thought, I'm living in the solution and I know this is where the possibility of a reunion with my son lives.

Much of this journey feels like I'm on a moving train winding my way along the sharp twists and turns of life and my job is simply to stay in balance. The waves of emotions still come, especially near his birthday, the end of school year, and the holidays, and when I move his pictures around in the house. These moments always make me reminisce. The difference now is I can regain balance more easily. I rarely have the weight of those memories convincing me I deserved what happened.

I practice the lessons of managing the emotional waves (just like I learned with May in the square of grief). I've come a long way and it's easier to allow myself to have fun by taking hikes and being outdoors with friends. I have new interests in food, books, music, and films. I look for the things that inspire me and I try to not get caught in the need for perfection in life. I allow myself the grace of being imperfect and I acknowledge my hard work. I'm part of the solution by being more loving toward myself and others and this too has shown me how this attitude serves a purpose.

Even after the miles I've traveled both inward and out, I still sometimes get hung up on banishing all doubt. This is hard work for me even today. But I am aware of this stumbling block so when I begin to doubt, and I suppose everyone does from time to time, I look at doubt and ask it to please find someone else to pester, or at the very least watch me from afar.

I knew in order for me to fulfill this spiritual assignment I would have to let go of my feelings of inadequacy even if it was only minutes at a time. I continued to release more diversions and procrastination and through this I've become more comfortable and alive. I had to practice sitting still and writing in increments of fifteen minutes at a time. I prayed to *God* for the courage and clarity to excavate and write the story that is one of glory.

I wanted to leave a trail of evidence that change is possible for other parents and children to see. I wanted them to know they too can make it through. Many parents and children have reached out through my blog, *Never Give Up Mom*. I believe we are all looking for ideas that will help us so we can reunite. *Love* is the universal language for all of us. Stories of reunion give hope to those who desire a loved one to return to them. Reconciliation, reunion, and hope all pave the way for people who desire a deep connection in their life.

Throughout this project I've continued to ask for the words and ideas that would resonate with people, whether they are parents or not. I received the idea that everyone was once a child and that transcends all cultures, religions, and societies.

I knew I was executing my purpose, but I often struggled to stay on one topic or would judge a topic as unimportant. Every time I let doubt creep in and stay too long I was reminded again, *"Tell them about you, and let them see me through your journey."*

Writing my story hasn't been easy but it has been a rich and intimate spiritual experience. Writing this book continues to connect me to my son, and pull me forward enjoying more purpose. It has moved me into the meaning phase of life, as Dr. Wayne Dyer stated in his film *The Shift*. I have arrived with more empathy for others and an awareness that I want to be of service.

I no longer feel pain when I identify as a mother. When I was raising my son I almost exclusively identified as a mother and nothing else. There was no balance in this identity and I shut off the other parts of me such as artist, writer, female, athlete, horse lover, and so on. All of these other aspects of my identity gave me such *joy,* as did my mothering. If I didn't identify with all of me, how could I flourish? Our planet has more than just trees to make an environment—there are a multitude of components that make up the whole. When I no longer identified primarily as a mother, I felt I had no identity and was lost in a foreign world. But the same power that is at work in all of our lives whispered in my ear and said, *Charla, you are much more than a mother!* I lived for my son and I loved that, but I made him my only reason to live and *Spirit* all the while wanted so much more than that for me.

With my new identity forming and my purpose laid out I continued to open myself up to whatever came my way. This quote from Rumi crossed my path and summed up my experience of forward pull.

> *"Let yourself be silently drawn by the strange pull of what you really love. It will not lead you astray."* —Rumi

Engaging in something greater than myself gives me the courage to view this separation with my son differently.

> *"Goodbyes are only for those who love with their eyes. Because for those who love with heart and soul, there is no separation"* —Rumi

This energy loves me and demonstrates that we're all connected whether in the presence of each other or not. And going one step further, I've experienced this *Love* amid my deepest sorrow and pain. When God said *tell them about me,* I knew this gave me purpose through my pain.

Reflections: Finding Purpose in My Pain

From working with horses and experiencing their reactions to my grief, I understand that compassion for myself and others is key to healing loss. Is there something you can do for others today to make their day a little easier? Compassion and service for another puts you in a position of strength. What do you have that you no longer need and can throw out or give away? I find that clearing clutter from my home also helps to energetically clear the space in which I live so I can have the room for the birth of new possibilities. Clearing space of clutter and giving items to those who need them also puts you in a more empowered position.

What flavorful or healthy foods or new recipes can you bring into your diet? Caring for our bodies and being nice to ourselves are vital in becoming stronger.

All of the answers to these questions are life-giving. Serving others puts us in the position of strength, companionship, and knowing that we are needed. Giving away what we no longer need or want frees us of old things and the past. Maybe you want to keep something for the sentimental value. Great! I have found when I let go of anything there is something or someone ready to come in and fill that space. The opportunity of being the empty vessel, or closet for that matter, makes way for better things. Changes in our thinking give us access to new opportunities for creating a healthier self, and with that the clarity to lead more inspiring lives. There is a purpose in our pain. I guarantee that.

CHAPTER 8

WALK IN BEAUTY

With beauty before me may I walk
With beauty behind me may I walk
With beauty above me may I walk
With beauty all around me,
may I walk...
—Taken from *A Navajo Prayer*

Before I left for Santa Fe, New Mexico, in December 2013, I had only known this town as a stop for tourism and recreation. Decades before, I had come to indulge in its inviting restaurants and shops, be entertained by the Santa Fe Opera Company, and enjoy myself on its many incredible ski slopes. Even as a visitor, I felt this place was completely different than any other city I traveled to. It is one of the oldest capital cities in the country, founded by the Spanish colonists in 1610. The city's full name when founded was La Villa Real de la Santa Fe de San Francisco de Asis, which translates as *The Royal Town of the Healing Faith of St. Francis of Assisi*. The Spanish now refer to it as the town of *Holy Faith*. In this place filled with a mystical spirit, I began an inward journey to reveal and relinquish beliefs about myself that continued to paralyze me and prevent me from living my life to its fullest.

On my quest in Santa Fe, I met Pasha Hogan, a phenomenal Reiki master and yoga teacher, author, and healer. Her message to me was one of rebirth. I went to her yoga class early in the morning, walking through the frigid, barren landscape to meet with her in a room that overlooked a snowy mesa. My journey had taken me to the middle of nowhere it seemed, but this was where I needed to be to leave behind what was still burdening me. I knew soon after arriving that I was supposed to be there, in the desolate desert to live in its silence. I needed to hear and see the truth of the thorns buried deep in my heart. I needed to do this sacred surgery so I could step off the path of deep sorrow. I took this time to put my life in order and birth a new perspective. Instead of sorrow, I came to feel a deep gratitude that I had traveled that far and, in every way, *I was standing.* Standing in that room waiting for her, I felt that I was in a womb, working hard to rearrange all the pieces that had made me. I wanted to clear out false memories and give my brokenness a place to heal.

After several weeks of Pasha's encouraging tutelage, I was integrating the sacred nature of this practice and felt myself changing from worthless to worthy, from broken to whole. My awareness of the stigma and judgment that went along with the loss of my son was beginning to lessen its hold on my mind and around my heart.

I no longer wanted to move my body only in order to look and feel good—I had to move out of the wasteland I had been navigating. I was learning the art of self-acceptance through yoga. Pasha's instruction was comprehensive and encouraging, yet gentle, and in every move I made alongside her, I awakened the *sleeping beauty* within me. I started to feel something in me that I had unconsciously buried long ago. It was my feminine self. Even though I took the time to apply my makeup every day, and felt such a passion for beauty, I realized I used my makeup skills to show up as a pretty female but not embrace that part of me. I hadn't connected the dots until now. I looked the part but in essence I was acting in order to receive acceptance from the world. My feminine self-had been buried by years of sorrow and sadness. But being in Santa Fe, willing to construct timelines of my life in order to see the truth about it, was the process of reclaiming all of me. I knew I no longer just wanted to *appear* a woman; I wanted to *embody* all of *HER*.

In an art class one day, Pasha shared her story with us and her journey from being a three-time cancer survivor to a woman who created healing circles and retreats filled with creative discovery in order to help others explore their healing process. She started the class by sharing a poem titled *The Journey*, written by Mary Oliver. As she read the poem I knew I had never heard anything so powerful, delivered by someone who personified the message in the poem. It sent chills through my body, because I had come to the end of allowing myself to be on the wrong road. The decision to walk away from prior beliefs and lies that no longer served me was critical, and to honor the story that brought me here was holy.

The call to action Pasha asks of her students and followers is simply to know that we are worth the risk of walking on the unknown road of change. We are worthy of being free from past constraints and we are righteous in wanting to live our lives healed and whole. As I listened, I knew in my gut that I came here to make this decision to "walk on," whatever may come—even if this meant the most inconceivable thought, moving farther away from my son.

When she finished reading the poem I knew I had come to this remote snowy mesa to find my voice again. And as my silence came to an end, I saw the sweetest part of me begin to take shape and rise.

It was time to be present in the process of integrating my entire journey and writing my story from this point forward. I engaged fully in gatherings and groups I came upon and one day I found a creative group that referred to their meeting as "core." This group had created a sacred cocoon in order to reveal their core stories and to be witnessed and supported by others without judgment. Here I found out that my dark secrets weren't always mine alone. They were other people's errors in life as well, but I had punished myself for these lies and misconceptions. This was the most profound course I have ever engaged in and because of this I learned new ways of loving myself.

We were asked to write a fairy tale and use the archetypes that we studied as characters in our new life story. Two years after writing this "Fairy Tale," I'm embodying that tale and my life is living proof that you too can write your own story and live a life of your choosing.

January 2014   **Fairy Tale**

Once upon a time there was a very healthy baby girl with blue eyes and dark hair who was born to a young woman who had no care from others and much abuse in her life.

The young woman told her daughter why she couldn't keep and raise her. She was young and pregnant and she was dropped off and abandoned by her love, the father of the baby, sexually abused by her stepfather, then turned away by her mother.

She had only two choices—to abort the baby or give birth to her. She obviously chose the latter and so their journey together began, as fighters. The mother's fight was to grow the baby and keep them both alive, and the baby's, after being born, was to survive being given up for adoption and to keep on fighting on her own. As the baby lay in a crib by herself, she felt isolated and desolate, with very little company and input from others.

Eventually, when the new family came to get her, she had already begun to understand the necessity of counting on herself and the complexity of survival.

The Kingdom she went to live in was communal, kind, and distant all at the same time. As any baby, puppy, or pony would, she craved closeness and was left hungry for it throughout her childhood. At the age of ninety-two, the mother who had raised her said "You practically raised yourself from the time you were four." That was a young age to take the reins of one's life, but a necessity for survival and growth.

As she grew into adolescence she called upon the Warrior to be a part of her as she watched violence, guns, gangs, and injustice around her. She felt compassion for those more afraid than she was, and weaker in constitution and spirit. With the Warrior in place another aspect of herself emerged: the Heroine. With her the girl was able to speak out and invite consciousness to lead the way in witnessing the violence in her neighborhood. She ran for student body leadership positions hoping to steer her peers to fruitful, productive, and fulfilling lives at school. The little Warrior/Heroine at home desperately wanted the attention of her parents because she knew her neighborhood and school were about to explode with violence and she was marked as one to hurt. Her parents were first unable to respond but when they finally did, she successfully convinced them where to move and it was good.

The Poet and Artist now emerged and she found her first love—Beauty—in the film and fashion business. She worked diligently for the first five years at her art and craft. Eventually, after many miles and many years of photo shoots, locations, and celebrities, she achieved her professional dream of being managed by an Artist agent, being called part of the "A" team, in the elite circle of her peers. She traveled to remote and exotic places around the globe. Her work and purpose were fruitful.

She, the Artist, came into contact with her love for poetry, and met a tall, dark, and handsome stranger who became her rock, husband, and father to her only child. At this time she collapsed in her life with a condition that had no physical diagnosis. What it took from her was all of her confidence in her belief that she was healthy and unstoppable. Then the rock she had married became an anchor chained to her soul and within four years of her marriage, she was forced to wake up to the death of it. She cut the chain off and swam to the top of the black ocean before she and her baby drowned the ugliest of deaths.

The Heroine and Protector emerged, swam away with the baby, and began to understand how the Provider would take center stage into their lives. At this time the Goddess appeared and with the swift nature of a flowing stream, covered the rough exteriors of the Heroine, Warrior, Fighter, and Protector, and made all things in her world Beautiful. It was something she truly enjoyed doing for herself and others and she made her exterior world, and herself, a flawless palette, while keeping her worn interior safe and sound. Eventually her interior, *though well masked, found its way through the cracks and became visible again. Her worn and fragile nature came bursting through and with that her anger, resentment, and fear, and it dissolved the Goddess. The joy, sensual curiosity, and self-esteem that had flowed freely from her disappeared. She was once an oracle of hope, passion, and perseverance, but these turned to hopelessness, gloom, and futility. The worst was not over and in the decade to come, she found herself running for her life, her love, and her survival in every earthly way.*

Eventually, a clearing appeared in the thick fog, revealing what stood alone. All of her. All of the Goddess, Warrior, Artist, Poet, Fighter, Protector, and Provider stood there shredded down to the bone. All else had been torn away.

The Artist had become so skilled that this part of her immediately took the lead. This is the part of her that brought her and her creations to life. The Artist would wield her brushes, blend her colors, and use any surface to create a new, stable, and meaningful world so that the Goddess in her could be wrapped in love and joy.

To endure the re-fleshing process, the Goddess and Artist solicited the Warrior within. Knowing the endurance the Warrior possessed, they asked the Warrior to engage in her highest form of power, which is gentleness and compassion. They knew that all creatures responded willingly to this kind of energy and intent. It was then that the Peaceful Warrior, born out of fire and life experiences, would be integrated in the re-fleshing of herself.

In order for this process to be complete she had to stay on the path much like an arrow that was being aimed and shot toward the center of a mark. In this manner the process allowed healing ways, safe choices, and inspiring events to take place.

As she continued to be re-fleshed, the Heroine emerged with a clearer vision for her future. Then the Provider, even more skilled, drew to herself the people and events she would need to complete this process and make sure there was a purpose in her painful journey.

The White Stallion that had been in her dreams became real to her and a carrier of the message of wisdom and power. The White Stallion came to tell her that she had made this journey to heal herself, as well her "brother and sisters" with the same pain. The White Stallion went on to say, "As I carry you upon my back, you will carry the needs of the people on yours. In gaining wisdom, you understand that power is not given lightly, but awarded to those who are willing to carry responsibility in a balanced manner." He finished by saying, "True Power is wisdom found in remembering your total journey."

All aspects of herself—Goddess, Peaceful Warrior, Artist, Mother, Provider, Protector, and Heroine—came together like a swirling vapor, and she relaxed with those she loved including her beloved son. They watched as the sunset invited them to enjoy their reunion at the close of this beautiful day and they lived happily ever after.

The End

As I prepared to leave Santa Fe to go home, I carried new dreams for my future. All of the healers, instructors, and friends I had met there helped me to see the beauty in my life and dismiss, for the last time, the burdens that were never mine in the first place. As I walked through the corridor to my gate at the Albuquerque airport, I saw one more *Divine* message for me in the form of a most amazing sculpture—an Indian shaman with an eagle. The name of the piece was *Dream of Flight* by artist Lincoln Fox. I walked closer to the statue to read the plaque. The inscription was memorable:

> *The dream of flight is born within the heart of man, embracing the desire to be free from the confines of the earth's surface. Hopefully the dream includes the possibility of freedom from limiting thought and action. As our imagination is freed to receive greater truths, then fear, closed thinking, and poverty of spirit will be left behind ... far below.*

The statue's spirit ushered me to my gate with its message of the freedom that I had attained and the assurance that my dreams were taking flight. As I boarded my plane for San Francisco I knew that they already were.

Reflections: Walk in Beauty

Beauty is easy, freedom loving, strong, and unstoppable. When I spend time with the horses they are all of these. There is nothing more powerfully beautiful than watching them run. There is nothing more inspiring than watching them converse and play with each other. Nothing more soulful than having one of them want to be near you, around you, carry you on their back. They live in idyllic outdoor settings even if the conditions are harsh.

I have been a part of beauty all of my life and so have you no matter what your story is. When you find yourself not walking in beauty, open the door of your mind, open the door of your home, and go for a walk. Open the doors of your closets, pantries, and vanities.

Make beauty on your face. Try a different way of applying your lipstick, try a different color. Try it with a different outfit.

Move the furnishings of your home around. Go shopping for something updated and beautiful for yourself and your surroundings. It doesn't have to cost a lot, but it does have to be outstanding.

Go for a walk, a run, or a ride in a beautiful setting and immerse yourself in all that surrounds you. Breathe in the sweet air; really look at the lush landscape. Focus on one beautiful thing and walk. Walk in the *beauty* of your *dreams*.

CHAPTER 9

ROOTS AND WINGS

"There are only two lasting bequests we can hope to give our children. One of these is roots; the other, wings."
—W. Hodding Carter II

I was given this quote in a blue frame as a gift at my baby shower more than eighteen years ago. It was written by a man I had never heard of before, but his gift and message about *Roots and Wings* resonated with me. It was important to me that I give my son experiences in his life that would allow him to grow and have a sense of roots. I read many parenting books and was always aware of the most current information, doctors' opinions, and trends. I wanted to raise my son properly, and often perfectly. I joined a moms group so I could observe and learn from other mothers and see if there was something I could do better. I also needed a community to share my experiences with and I felt there was no better group than new mothers. I wanted to be the best mom I could be because I had been waiting to have a child all my adult life. I knew that it was likely he would be my only child so I put everything else aside so I could to focus on mothering, nesting, and the creation of our family.

I saved several gifts from my baby shower hoping to give them to him one day. But this framed quote of *Roots and Wings* was a gift more for me than for my son. I saw it as a *Divine Message* and put it in the special box of family pictures and mementos. Throughout the last seven years of this separation I've had hundreds of questions about how I was as his mother. I dug up memories and pictures that I kept in a wooden box as I searched for answers to some of them. I've asked myself these questions: Did I do enough to give my son a sense of roots? Did I give him the experiences that would help him know how much I love him? And if so, did this help to ground him and make him feel more self-assured before he was taken? What did I give him in his formative years to help him to know he has all he needs to grow up into the person of his choosing? While I asked these questions and reminisced about his early years, I dismissed the blame that naturally arises in this situation. I no longer allowed the anger to take up too much space in my mind or for any length of time—anger isn't my constant companion any longer. When I start to bring up the circumstances that led to my son's abduction, I'm aware of the negative feelings and, just like turning off a light switch, I do the same to those feelings as quickly as possible. If I'm having a conversation about it, I find something else to discuss or I do something else more helpful or meaningful for me. I am reminded after a lot of practice that I don't want to go to the dark side of this situation anymore.

I have let go of many other items from my son's baby years but maybe my *soul* knew I would need to be reminded that I did give him opportunities to grow *roots* in our time together. When it comes to the subject of *wings,* some of us have had to use them much earlier in our lives than others and long before many parents would have preferred us to. I believe we are all born with *wings,* and just as I had to get to know this as a baby when I was given up for adoption, he would get to know his at the age of eleven when he was stolen from me.

When I began this journey to save myself from further harm, I was able to recall memories along the way that showed me that I did give my son experiences that may have rooted our time together in his mind and heart. The first of these memories was a little lullaby that came to me while driving into San Francisco.

I was about eight months pregnant and felt very peaceful in this part of my pregnancy, and I still had enough energy to keep working. It's hard to explain to anyone who has never given birth, but at the eight-month point mother and baby know each other well and the bond for me was *pure togetherness*. When I went to work I had to get myself mentally organized and I always felt it was the two of us going to work, not just me. I was experiencing such harmony in my life that as I drove a song came to me. The melody danced in my mind, and then the words blended right in. This was the first lullaby I sang for him before he was born and it lived on long after I brought him home from the hospital. This became one of the first examples of giving him roots.

I love you baby boy oh yes I do

I love you sweetheart and I'll be true

When you're not near me I'm blue

Oh baby boy I love you

I learned that unborn babies know their mother's voice and I hoped this catchy little tune I sang to him would make sure he'd know mine.

I remembered the times I put my son in a backpack and went for long walks and hikes in our neighborhood. Our home was a few blocks away from acres of open land with well-worn paths that wound through hillsides filled with giant oak trees.

My son was born with colic so the long walks lulled him to sleep and that gave me some peace even though I had to keep walking in order to keep him quiet. In the height of the summer heat and his crying I would put him in his car seat and drive to a coffee place, get a large iced coffee, put on the air conditioning, and drive up the highway for hours. The motion of the car and the humming of the engine gave him what he needed to sleep and it gave me some quiet time with him. I sipped my iced coffee, glancing at his precious face as he slept in the back seat. I put on soft music and we were both at peace.

As he became a toddler, and his walking turned quickly to running, our favorite places were parks and the hillsides in our neighborhood. I wanted to share my love for the outdoors with him, just as my dad did with me.

My dad was an outdoorsman and loved to find beautiful places where we could go camping. Once our campsite was set up, we went hiking and fishing. I grew up being very close to my dad and was definitely considered a daddy's girl. I would follow him everywhere as we trekked through the mountains and streams looking for the best places to fish and relax.

Among my most cherished memories is the time my dad asked me to come along with him and his buddies and all of their sons on a hunting trip in the Sierras. I was eight, and the only girl, and I was going with them to track deer in the snow! I knew my dad had enough confidence in me to ask me along and he knew I had enough *gumption* to say yes to his invitation. I always felt we were kindred spirits and it seemed natural that I was the one going with him instead of my brother. I had a feeling he was counting on me not to let him down and to show the rest of the guys that I could do what they were doing. We took off and hiked for miles in the snowy mountains.

It was an arduous trek even for my dad, but I was learning how to traverse the terrain with him by my side, sometimes slowly and sometimes filled with doubt. We were at the rear of the pack of all the other men and their sons, but it didn't matter to me because I was with my dad.

I learned on that trip that I could finish a trek with the men, but more important was the confidence I acquired, which allowed my roots to grow deeper. I learned that if I took my time, followed my lead (at that time it was my dad), tapped into my intuition, mapped out a course, and never gave up, I would eventually make it through and return back home. This is my mantra for life, with one more addition—*take the time to enjoy your journey.*

That adventure gave me the gift of confidence in myself to know I am wise enough to chart a path and to course correct when I need to. Feeling my dad's confidence in me helped me forge a strong bond with him throughout our lives and I know it was as special to him as well. I know his love of the outdoors transferred to me and I wanted to share this gift with my son. But this time I wanted to remember to enjoy the journey with my son, knowing how fast time passed. I had also looked forward to seeing my son build his confidence by introducing him to different outdoor experiences. I was excited for us to become fellow adventurers.

When my son was five we went for a hike at one of our local parks. It had been raining but the sun was trying to come out. I parked and saw one of the fire trails, so we headed off to see where it went. As we walked I saw a narrow path off the trail that led up toward the top of the hillside. I assumed the view had to be beautiful because the altitude was high enough to see the Pacific Ocean. I didn't know if we should attempt it since it had been raining and was still sprinkling a bit. Normally the trails were solid clay but the rain had turned them to mud in places. I knew if we made it to the top it would be an incredible accomplishment and we would feel like we were standing on the top of the world. Just as my dad took me on the many hikes in the Sierras and other locations, I wanted to take my son. He was a little younger than I was when I started hiking but I knew he was up to the challenge. Step by step, taking the climb slowly, charting our course, we would make it to the top. I felt my dad's spirit with us and I couldn't help but feel that this experience would impart the same confidence to his grandson as it did to me.

I had some trepidation when we started and I tried not to seem too nervous, but I suspect that was the same way my dad had felt about me. I took the lead and held onto my son's hand and we climbed up carefully. It was muddy and quite steep, so I asked him to follow behind me and stop when he got tired.

Once we were hiking and climbing, I never felt we were in any danger and, just like my dad did with me, I spoke to him in a calm voice and encouraged him to take his time, at his pace, and I would walk alongside him on the parts of the trail that were wide enough to do so. My hand held his at times and other times just gently touched him when I had confidence he was doing fine on his own. We eventually reached the end of the trail at the top of the hill. The rain was a bit heavier, and as I took the last step off the trail and onto the grassy knoll, I saw the sky widen into the Pacific Ocean. I gasped at the view and with one more tug I pulled my son up and onto the hill next to me. We stood there in the rain in our muddy shoes with our arms wrapped around each other, looking in amazement at how far we had hiked to what seemed like the top of the world. This was quite an experience in his young life and there would be many more adventures like this one to come.

Another time we sailed to the island of Catalina with friends for a weekend, staying with them on their boat. We anchored in a small cove offshore. It was a magical, sunny time with other boats coming in for their weekend getaways. Just as I wanted to show my son how to climb the hillside on that rainy day, I wanted to share the same type of experience with him at sea. I loved to swim and I had been a competitive swimmer in school, but I rarely got the chance to swim in the ocean off the back of a boat.

Our boat was moored about fifty yards off the shore of the island. I wanted to take a swim and asked my son if he wanted to go with me. He knew how to swim but had never ventured off a boat to swim to an island with other boats anchored all around us. This swim was a bit of an obstacle course and I had to pay attention to the other boaters and to him, all the while making our way toward shore. My son wanted to come and although I knew it would be a little challenging, I mapped out the course for our swim while we stood on the top deck of the boat.

I instructed him to swim next to me while I did the sidestroke next to him. I told him about the course we would take and of the obstacles to look for while we made our way to shore. I did a side dog paddle while he did a great job with freestyle as we made our way through the boats and the currents. As we swam, I kept my eyes peeled, watching for any signs of distress from him or changes in another boater's location. When we felt a surge in the water, I slowed our pace so we could correct our course and let the current push us instead of our working against it. When it seemed that we had been swimming for a while and the shore was too far away, we treaded water, regrouped, and swam again for the shore. I was a confident swimmer and the ocean felt familiar to me, and I hoped he was feeling the same way. I knew if he could experience climbing a hillside on a rainy day and swim to the shore of an island, he would have the experience of engaging with the outdoors with the knowledge that he had what it takes to go the distance.

The adventures I had with my dad were invaluable. They gave me insight into my strengths and desires to take chances and helped shape my character. And they gave me memories that I still cherish. I loved sharing the calming influence of the outdoors with all its beauty, as well as the challenges of the adventures. Even when the hikes, swims, or climbs were hard, and the outcome was unknown, I was better off having experienced them. My wish for my son is that when he reminisces about our adventures together, he also feels accomplished, strong, and rooted.

Letting go and seeing our babies take their first steps is exciting, but seeing them take flight encompasses a whole other set of emotions. When I'm around the horses I observe mares with their foals and how they are fiercely protective. In my volunteer work with an equine nonprofit group called Access Adventure, I was helping administer medication to the horses. One of them was a mare that had given birth a few weeks prior. Squeezing the syringe of medication into the mouth of a large Friesian horse is tricky enough, but doing this with a mare that had just given birth is even more difficult. One of us held her lead rope through the fence while the other two people administered the medication. We had only a handful of seconds once we had her mouth open to administer the de-worming mixture.

We had just finished when she pulled her head away to see where her baby was. When she saw her baby was being approached by one of our other volunteers, her body shook as she lifted her right leg up and started to paw and growl. I'd heard a horse make that sound once before but with this mare it was frightening. We watched her as she bobbed her head and pulled her lead rope away no matter the cost to herself or anyone else, to go after the person that was getting close to her baby. Her foal was using his *wings* to explore the other side of the ring with the volunteer, but this mare's protective nature was getting ready to attack. The director of the operation saw this and yelled to the volunteer to quickly get away from the foal.

I know in my case with my son, I always felt this way, and when I witnessed the mare's stance and manner I understood her fierce protection completely. She could have done so much damage to the volunteer if the director had not diffused the situation. I thought about what happened all the way home from the ranch and the other examples of mares being separated from their babies in order to wean them. The cries of the mares being separated from their foals are seared in my memory. This forced separation with the ability to still see her colt was almost too much for this mare.

I think back to the decision I made to leave my son and how it felt. It was the most painful decision I've ever made. I felt like these mares. Horrified to let go and terrified for my son and his welfare if I continued to fight in the courts. But my decision to leave and save my life was an act of growing *my w*ings. I had to take flight because I knew if I didn't, I'd never be the example for him that I wanted to be and I'd never have lived my life the way the *Divine* intended it to be. I wanted to be responsible for my *soul's journey.*

I knew there were no guarantees to seeing him again, but nevertheless, I had to fly. I had very little guidance in growing my wings but I knew it was necessary. The process has been painful and there have been more changes than I ever could have conceived of making, but I have been successful as long as I remain in the present and not the past.

I realized there was still something that tethered me to the remaining feelings of grief and my longings to be with my son again. I had dug deep and done years of therapeutic work. I had made supernatural advances in freeing myself, my wings, and my heart. But there was still something else that needed to be done to completely free me. One night while I was asleep, I was given this poem as a gift from my son's heart.

Don't blame yourself for all that happened
Don't blame yourself for what you could not do,
Be glad for I have grown up and I know you're proud of me too.
I can see, I can read every little word you've written—
And soon you'll know all the answers to your questions,
So set your heart free to be everything you have always wanted to be.
I want you to go on and dream
I want you to never stop being who you really are
For you have always been my shining star—
We will see each other again, it's only a matter of time
So until then love yourself
Voyage to your heart's content
I'll meet you where the words are heaven sent.

I woke up to write the words down and without any doubt I knew this sentiment came from him. I was now confident about a reunion, be it here on earth or some on other plane, and about his feelings about me. His gift allowed my breathing to return to normal; my shoulders relaxed and I released the past as I hadn't done before.

Reflections: Roots and Wings

All of us wrestle with our issues of roots and wings, whether we have acquired deep strong roots from our families or we grew our own. And at some point, we will all have to process the act of growing our wings, whether when our children leave the nest or when loved ones pass into the next realm. This is human existence.

What do you need to attend to? Your roots or wings? Do you sway easily to external forces and desire more stability?

Are you wrestling with letting go of someone or something that is no longer in your home or here on this plane of existence?

Give yourself time and be compassionate with yourself because it takes time to grow a strong root system and it takes courage to let someone go.

There is a quote written by Guillaume Apollinaire that symbolizes the journey we all will take.

"Come to the edge," he said.
"We can't, we're afraid!" they responded.
"Come to the edge," he said.
"We can't, we will fall!" they responded.
"Come to the edge," he said.
And so they came.
And he pushed them.
And they flew.
— Guillaume Apollinaire

CHAPTER 10

DARE TO DREAM

Reach high, for stars lie hidden in your soul. Dream deep,
for every dream precedes the goal.
—Pamela Vaull Starr

It was three a.m. and I was jolted out of bed. It felt as if my son had reached out from his world to mine. The dream was so vivid and the events so real that I raced to my computer to jot down the details. Maybe the dream was prompted by a Brendon Burchard conference which I had attended several days earlier. That event had invigorated me and the four days there were filled with inspiring stories from people from all over the world. I met people from as far away as Cambodia. This was the largest group with the most cultural diversity I had ever engaged with. Our differences were great, but so was our *hunger* to lift our lives to a higher level of living and engage fully with those we loved. I came away from this event feeling elevated and sensing that something *big* was right around the corner.

I had adopted Burchard's mantra: Have I lived, loved, and mattered? I certainly knew I had lived and had made deep inroads into living a happier life in the past few years. Had I loved? Without question, I knew that I had, especially with the creation of the *Never Give Up Mom* blog. Have I mattered? Yes. I had built a bridge of love, made from hours of words and years of work, for my son and for other parents and children who have experienced the same rupture of a relationship. I had found a way to preserve my son's childhood with pictures of him and my side of the family to view if he ever found the blog. After my own financial crash, I had once again bought a home. In it, I had prepared a room for my son, hoping and praying that one day he would search for me and return to his mom.

My life felt steady and I was firmly planted on this new ground. In my dream I had a sense that both of us wanted to come together. I believed that as he grew older and matured, he became more independent of the people who had made choices for him in the past. I also believed that he had begun to make his move toward me too. Gregg Braden's story of the separation of matter flashed through my mind, followed by pictures of places my son and I use to go, and memories of how I met my birth parents and the events that led to that. I remembered the years and distance that separated us and the day that I met both of them. There were people and events that drew us together but mainly it was my intention to find them and to never give up until I did. I've experienced both of these separations and now I had watched my reunion with my son in the dream.

This reconnection was possible; I had the proof. I just needed to believe it. I needed to use the power I had. I needed to focus, stay intentional and hopeful, and trust that the result of a reunion will come in God's time and way.

The memory of standing in the square of reunion rushed into my mind, and then the horses galloping toward us. I remembered our imaginary reunion with the horses looking over the fence and Dr. Lambert's amazement at this sight.

I remembered what I had been asking for all along: *A safe place where we could meet, and on our own ground and terms of our making. A place that was open and comfortable so we could give each other plenty of room to calm down and come together. A place that a dream would provide.*

I could no longer deny this feeling of being pulled toward him. It wasn't just in my mind, it was a physical sensation. There were many times I thought I saw an outline of a person float by me out of the corner of my eye, like a ghost. I was familiar with entities, angels, and images of light moving past me and now I saw them more frequently. I thought about him daily, but these weren't just thoughts any longer. I felt his presence, his will, and his curiosity to know me. I have imagined hundreds if not thousands of times what it would be like to see my son again—to be able to relax together in each other's presence. To observe him with happiness and pride the way I had done for his whole life when he was with me. This dream was out of context since I typically don't have dreams or ones that I can remember. I never imagined that this would take place in a dream!

It was October 2015, the month of my son's eighteenth birthday. A very big year for him and for me. I couldn't make sense of this feeling that *he* was trying to reach me. My intuition was heightened and I was experiencing the same feelings I'd had before, when we lived together. I was a tuned-in parent and sometimes I knew what my son was going to do before it even happened.

When I opened my computer to start writing it was 3:34 a.m., I had been tossing and turning until this dream unfolded in precise detail and clarity as if it were real.

In my dream I arrived at an arcade that we used to visit years ago. I spent many hours there with my son and his friends at parties and gatherings. As I walked through the door of the arcade I felt like I was at a high altitude and a little oxygen deprived, resulting in a floating feeling. I remember thinking why am I here? I knew I didn't live in that city anymore and my son was no longer a little boy. I continued to make my way through the arcade and I reminisced about the games I had played with him and his friends. I smiled at the sight of all the bright flashing lights and the pinging sounds and remembered all the fun times we'd had there.

I turned the corner and walked past a group of kids screaming as someone was playing one of the games. I stopped for a moment to see what they were all watching and as my eyes shifted I spotted my son! He definitely wasn't a little boy—he had grown into a teenager. This was the first time I had seen him in seven years. I was as shocked in the dream as I am sure I would be in real life.

He looked up from the crowd, straight at me as if he knew I was going to be there. In this millisecond of time his eyes softened and they told me that he knew about my efforts to reach him through my blog. He gazed at me for a second longer and I accepted his acknowledgement. He then looked away and went back to watching the game.

Without hesitation I moved through the crowd. I no longer felt the burden of guilt. I no longer hungered to know how he was. My prayers were answered and the sorrow vanished. Because of this release I didn't have to fall prey to self-loathing. I had just witnessed in my dream a reconciliation of our relationship. A new life had begun even if it was just in a dream.

I now understood that this new hunger I had for a connection with my son was not born from the past, but from the intent to meet each other where we are now in our lives.

My desire drove me to continue walking through this arcade of possibility. I felt strong and sure of myself. I didn't know where my son went or if I would see him again. I saw the open doors that led to the patio and I headed for them. Right before I left the arcade I turned to take one last look around and as I did I saw him again. It felt like only a few minutes since we had acknowledged each other but this time he was older and stronger and more alert to my presence. He had grown into a young man! He didn't face me with the same wide-eyed gaze, but he acknowledged me and as he did the corners of his mouth turned up slightly into a warm smile. He seemed open, even relaxed with the idea of my being in the same room with him. He turned away to play another game with his friends and I walked outside into another space of the dream.

I felt the pangs of physical hunger now. I entered the crowded patio and saw the miniature golf course I had played on many times before and heard the buzzing sounds of the go-carts. I knew that the only place I could get something to eat was at the hot dog stand. But as I looked around I didn't see it. It had changed. In the blink of an eye the familiar patio area had changed into an outdoor marketplace. I made my way through the crowds and the aroma of cooking in all the kitchens enveloped my senses and time slowed. I walked up to a food stand serving sandwiches and breathed deeply with my eyes closed, inhaling the scent of fresh fish and french fries. My mouth was watering, imagining how good my meal was going to taste. I opened my eyes, and as I did the busy crowd in front of me slowed down and then began to clear. I saw a man standing and facing me about five feet away. He was tall with broad shoulders and dark hair, and he was looking straight at me. Oh my God, It's him, it's my son! *I looked straight into his beautiful brown eyes and in a moment I witnessed his growth from birth to now. I stared at his full face and smiling mouth. He was looking straight at me, his* MOM.

I thought to myself while staring back at him with wonder, He's here! He came and made it through his hurt, his confusion, and pain. He traversed his obstacles, uncertain of the outcome.

At that moment he was as hungry for communication with me as I have been all these years. I stared at him wondering what I should say but in my first words, Hello son, how are you? *a lifetime of wondering about him vanished. I asked him if he wanted to sit and have a meal with me and he replied,* Yes. *So I walked up to the counter and ordered two dinners of fish sandwiches, fries, and drinks. I picked up our dinner and we found a large white table away from the crowd. As we sat down, the noise hushed. I didn't hear anything around us. This was a sacred moment as we sat and shared our first meal together in seven years and it symbolized a holiday gathering to me. I remembered all the meals I had with him, from his first bite of solid food to now. They were all special but this meal was magical. Our physical hunger and the hunger of our hearts were satisfied and we enjoyed this meal like no other. This dream gave us a place to come home to each other.*

It was 4:43 am. I sat at the dining room table, staring at my computer screen, and realized I just witnessed a dream writing itself through me. I was reeling from this experience and in awe of the story that came bursting through. I was feeling all the physical sensations in my body and especially in my heart. I felt as if I'd seen my son for the very first time in seven years and we were able to share the same time and space together. This dream of floating through our memories and allowing each other to mature, sitting down to eat, and picking up our relationship from where we are now, changed everything for me. I was given my heart's desire and I knew the heavens were on our side.

It was still dark outside. The house was silent. The room was cool and I felt weightless, just like in the dream. I headed back to my room, lay my head on the pillow, void of the excitement that woke me and fell asleep.

I lay my head down on the pillow and as I took a deep breath in and exhaled, so did every part of my body. In that moment I reconnected the part of me that I had left years before and I reveled in the knowledge that I *am* and have always been, my *son's mother*.

The dream that I dared to dream was real and the results were evident. I am a mother. I was there with him, and he was there with me. No more refuting this fact. This really happened. My intention changed from *if* to *when*. It was just a matter of time.

Reflections: Dare to Dream

I still had no physical evidence that I would see or hear from him again, but I had just walked out of a reunion with him on another plane of existence and I knew, beyond a shadow of a doubt, I would never be the same. *The Mother* in me came out of the shadow and took her rightful place in me.

What do you want to reconnect to in yourself? What part of you have you put away, forgotten about, or shut off?

I am of the belief that until you bring back the part of you that's hungering for engagement, engagement won't happen. Daring to dream is about reconnecting to the missing part of you that makes you whole.

I was engaged in my healing and as a result eventually came to the dream of reunion. In this instance it wasn't so much about the reunion between my son and me as it was about reclaiming my role as a mother.

I have played so many roles in my life and now the role of mother resides comfortably inside of me.

In the dream world the possibilities of reconnection are there waiting for you. What role do you want to reconnect with? Lover, woman, father, sister, artist, leader, writer, brother, teacher, entrepreneur, giver, inner child, or wholehearted human?

CHAPTER 11

"HEY MOM"

*Most of the important things in the world have been
accomplished by people who have kept on trying when there
seemed to be no hope at all.*
—Dale Carnegie

W hen I came upon the preceding quote more than a half decade ago, it caught my eye and reminded me to keep trying, knowing what I was attempting was *important.* I had seen this framed quote at one of my favorite retail stores so I bought it and took it home with me; it hung in my kitchen for a year before I moved to my new home. I had packed it in a box and planned to hang it in the room I prepared for my son, but had forgotten all about it until recently, when the day came that I needed to be reminded of that promise.

I knew this was the *Divine* speaking to me and I held onto this message of *hope* as if it were a life raft. I think about all the events that must have happened for Dale Carnegie to coin this phrase of courage and perseverance. Today I needed to be reminded of all I had accomplished up to this point and to remember that today my efforts will be enough.

I have seen God in so many disguises in the past seven years: horses, small jobs, sunrises and sunsets, synchronistic events, films, books, and meetings with many friends and healers who have passed my way. These things got my attention and something in me knew where the goodness in my life came from. My faith has grown immensely throughout these trials and years, yet I still discounted the words of friends when they said that my son would find me one day, once he was free to. I suppose I kept myself guarded to prevent further crushing disappointment. His eighteenth birthday came, and as I did every year, I hesitated. And then I got myself together emotionally and wrote one more blog post, hoping he would find it. For his birthday and for our celebrated holy day, Christmas, I would always repost those blog posts on my Facebook page and would ask others to join in his birthday celebration or leave him holiday wishes.

The year of his eighteenth birthday had a different feeling to it. My year had been one filled with wonder, freedom, and beauty. I'd had the opportunity to return to the work I was passionate about, and I'd fallen in love. It had been fruitful and sweet. There was only one thing missing—my son. I had become the best I'd ever been with my new normal. Even my affinity for technology had grown, and that was miraculous.

One morning I woke up, made tea, and began my day. I had my to-do list made and my home was filled with peace and the familiarity of my daily routine. I held the cup of hot green tea and smelled the fragrant lemongrass in it. I took a sip and set the cup down on the side of the sink. I planned to go for my morning walk and do my stretches in my favorite spot overlooking the bay, then head back up the hill and do the power portion of my walk back home. I was ready to go but I wanted to get my phone so I could listen to some music. I walked into the guest room to unplug my phone from the charger and saw something I had never seen before. There was an Instagram icon in the notification list on my phone, and next to the icon, my son's name!

I stared at the icon, then blinked my eyes several times. My mind was racing trying to make sense of this. I am an Instagram user but I didn't know that it had a messaging feature. I had never seen this before, and as I stared at it, I wondered if it was a hoax or if this really was my son contacting me? Finally, it registered that it must be my son! I screamed and was so excited in the moment I dropped the phone on the floor. I scrambled to the floor to pick it up as my partner came rushing into the room to see what all the commotion was about. He looked at me and asked, "What's going on? Are you okay?" I stood up, looked right at him, and with a smile said, "Look at this." I pointed to the icon with my son's name attached to it and as he read it his eyes widened. We looked at each other and our eyes filled with tears. I wrapped my arms around him and cried.

I couldn't believe the day had come. It was a *new normal* kind of morning and yet it wasn't at all.

As I reached for a tissue to wipe the tears from my face he held the phone and said, "Say something back to him."

I looked at the screen of the phone and read the words again. *Hey Mom.* I was frozen, not knowing what to say. So my darling helped me form my first sentence to my son. *Hi Son, how are you?* I began to type these simple words and in the few seconds it took for me to type them, *Spirit* reached through my fingers and I felt the pieces of my heart *reattach themselves.* I pressed send and exhaled air that seemed like it had been trapped in me for years. I felt the relief that only a reunion could produce and knew I was in the presence of *Grace.* I was astounded and overwhelmed and grateful for the fact we were both still alive and *he* had found me!

This first text from him came approximately fifty-two hours after he turned eighteen. I was elated about our communication, but I also felt unsure of myself. I had focused so much on the trauma of the past, that part of me continued to identify with that portion of the story as his mother. Now he was reaching out for me in the here and now, and I knew it was the opportunity I had been waiting for. It was time to allow the past to drift out of my being for good.

I know I will never forget what happened in the past, and that by honoring my whole story I could fully take my power back and be present as his mother. This was an act of liberation for me and the opportunity to step into my son's life again as I am today.

With the support of loving friends and experts in the realm of trauma and healing, I opened myself to wise voices that helped me realize that I *am* my son's mother and always have been. Their voices of support helped me solidify my renewed feelings of our reunion and it was music for my soul.

Over the next few weeks, as I shared my great news with a few select friends, I began to feel more connected in my relationship of mother and son. I was still in my head about all of this but I finally realized that the power of the *language of our hearts* brought us together. Once I had accepted this, it was as if I had climbed aboard a rocket and blasted away from all that had haunted me. It had been just a couple of weeks since I had received his message of encouragement and love in the form of a poetic dream and it had just come true!

In an instant, I remembered all of the dreams, messages, and passing thoughts I had received from him (or believed that they came from him) and I could see him charting his course as he walked through the multiverses of time on his path to me. He had traversed his terrain just as we had done more than a decade before on the muddy hillside of Southern California.

I turned to the screen on my phone to see if he had responded to my last message to him. He had written back, *Happy to hear from you too, wanted to let u know I've been reading your blogs.*

There it was. All the years of writing and pressing publish had made its way to him. With *Divine Love and Spirit, the way was made.* The invention of the Internet, Google, WordPress, and the Never Give Up Mom blog helped me build the bridge. The support and encouragement from Dr. Lambert, the horses, and many others helped me along this challenging and seemingly impossible path.

God hoped I would pray for the courage to keep a soft and open heart long enough to trust and follow the promptings to keep writing from my soul. The agony of the task morphed into relief and I acknowledged that writing from my heart was the highest form of love and communication I had to give.

In my next message I asked if it was safe for him to communicate with me. His answer: *Yeah of course I truly appreciate them* [my posts] *lots and its ok. I'm extremely busy with school and life and I'm very involved with sports... And I believe so I don't see why not I'm 18.*

His reply spoke volumes to me. I remembered the time he took his first bites of solid food as a baby and now he's telling me he is his own man. He has always known how to take care of the next steps in life and that he is up to the challenge and, most important of all, he is okay.

Several weeks after our initial contact continued to be my new reality, I remembered the vivid dream I had about seeing him in the arcade. That dream woke me up on October 4, 2016, and he contacted me on October 20, 2016. Was this dream given to me so I could prepare for the real reunion on this physical plane?

It was a portal I chose to walk through, and once through, was presented with several opportunities to respond to him in new ways. In remembering this dream it felt as if I had written this story before. This was a gift set in motion when I wrote my "Fairy Tale" a couple of years before.

On and off throughout my life, I've had experiences that have felt like something loving was caressing me. When I was that baby lying in a crib after being given up for adoption, there was a benevolent presence there with me. While I was walking on a trail on top of the barren, snowy mesa in Santa Fe, I felt something touch my cheek that I dismissed as the breeze, knowing it wasn't just that. There have been so many instances when the *Divine* met me right where I was. Even with my limited understanding, I knew I was experiencing something loving and profound.

Every moment I contemplated being in communication with my son and every unanswered question I asked in the past seven years was being validated and answered. I remembered the card I was given by a friend, with a message meant for me, when I arrived in Northern California at the beginning of this journey.

> *Be patient toward all that is unsolved in your heart and try to love the questions themselves, like locked rooms and like books that are now written in a very foreign tongue. Do not now seek the answers, which cannot be given you because you would not be able to live them. And the point is, to live everything. Live the questions now. Perhaps you will then gradually, without noticing it, live along some distant day into the answer.*—Rainer Maria Rilke

I recently came across the card again while looking through a box of pictures and keepsakes. The message resonated with me and I had a strong resistance to it at the same time. I didn't want to grow into the answers; I wanted to know them immediately. I wanted to get to point Z and not have to walk the path of the unknown, moving further away from where I started, and further away from my son. I didn't want the pain and the separation, but I understood that the sentiment of the card was probably true. I knew as I read that wisdom of the ages, that I had experienced this before with my birth grandmother.

There was an enormous rift in my birth family when I was given up for adoption. My paternal aunt told me this story on a Christmas Eve the year my grandmother turned eighty. When my grandmother found out that she couldn't do anything to change this situation for me, she cried and grieved for a full year. One day, with her family encouraging her to stop mourning for the loss, she finally did. Instead, she allowed herself to believe that, eventually, I would one day come knocking on her door.

Thirty-four years passed and through various means, including *the language of our hearts*, we reunited on a Christmas Eve. Her faith and perseverance, despite her family telling her to give up all hope of seeing me one day, prevailed. I was able to meet her and get to know her for several years before she passed away.

Throughout this journey I've called upon my paternal grandmother and my ancestors to watch over my son and keep him safe and my perseverance strong. My prayers have been answered and I have learned a lifetime of lessons along the way. One of the most important insights I had was that *it's not as important to see with your eyes as it is to feel with your heart.*

Today my son and I continue to communicate with each other in ways that are private. This allows us to get to know each other as we are today and to create the relationship of our choosing. When he texted me, he gave me the greatest gift I could have imagined: answers to so many unanswered questions. He crossed the bridge I built and I feel more relaxed in this next phase of our reunion. I'm hopeful for a close and loving relationship with him, without wanting to force any outcomes. The deepest longing to see him has faded, even though I would travel to see him anytime, anywhere.

When I walk past my favorite picture of him, I feel his presence and visualize seeing him, reaching up to hug him instead of reaching down. I feel the warmth of his body and the kind of relief that only a parent could experience after years of separation.

I believe, as my grandmother did with me, that he will come knocking on my door one day and we will sit and enjoy the presence of each other in a peace that surpasses all understanding.

Reflections: Hey Mom

YES! This was one of the happiest days of my life.

Did I pull this in? Did we both make this happen? In some ways, yes. Over the years I've had a number of people from my attorneys to friends, family members, and virtual strangers, praying for my son and me to reunite. There are no words for the gratitude I feel for all the time, energy, and prayers we've received.

Is there someone you would like to reach? Or, who are you waiting to hear from? Is this person still alive? I've experienced the thin veil between the worlds and the more communication you're engaged in, the more you'll feel the desire of your heart.

Don't wait if the desire you have has never faded. This means your hearts are still very much alive and through your hearts a connection can be built. Take the chance and be the one to reach out. You deserve to live your answers. Be bold!

CHAPTER 12
A PLACE OF PEACE

*Peace is all around us—in the world and in nature—
and within us—in our bodies, and our spirits. Once
we learn to touch this peace, we will be healed and
transformed. It is not a matter of faith;
It is a matter of practice.*
—Thich Nhat Hanh

I've touched this place of *Peace*. This place isn't born from logic or circumstances or doctrine and it always surpasses all understanding. I know this peace exists in the moment and not in a destination except one place—the redwoods in West Marin County, California.

I recently had the images of the redwoods in my dreams and then in my daily thoughts. I pay attention to repetitive thoughts these days because I know this is how the *Divine* works. These messages are usually calling me to go somewhere, make a call, or contact someone for a specific reason, or put a task at the top of my priority list. I've learned to be present to *God's* calling and not resist the ideas I'm presented with. The images I saw were of a familiar state park that I've visited many times.

Under a canopy of majestic redwoods, I starting writing my story over a half decade ago, though at that time I had no idea I was writing this book. At that time I wanted to visit a place that held happy memories for me and be comforted by them. Today I want to visit this same place and make new memories so I can bathe in the beauty that I often experience now.

This time I didn't make the drive alone. On the most heavenly of Sundays we drove over bridges as picturesque as a watercolor painting, breathed in the bay air, and made our way through the winding roads of the backcountry until we reached the magical redwoods of West Marin. Driving through this iconic area made me calm; my mind became slow and clear and any negative thoughts broke away and disappeared. As we drove into the state park, windows wide open, my eyes were fixated on the trees while the wind blew past my face and through my hair. The fragrance of enchantment was everywhere.

We entered the park where rangers came out to greet us with a smile, asking, *How long will you be staying with us?* Camping or day use were the choices and the rangers' welcome was as if you had come home and your family was happy you've arrived.

This time I wasn't going to reminisce about the past exclusively. I would point out the specific places within the park where the best s'mores were made, and where the redwood tree fairies hid among the ferns on the miles of meandering trails. This time I wasn't going to a space where I poured out my pain and suffering. I was going to thank the monolithic ancestors for their inspiration and strength. *I wanted to stand in the spot where I began my new life again.*

I was there with my sweetheart and partner, the man who knew my bitter story of the past and was in the deep end of love with me now. I knew I no longer needed to prove that I had made it through what had almost killed me. I no longer had to remain tied to the memories of the past. I stood in this spot where it all began, perfectly, wholly calm in the present.

I wanted to be beside the rushing river and thank her for her music of encouragement that many times was a lullaby for my soul. I wanted to listen to her as we walked and explored new places on the trails of her banks. I wanted to thank her for the peace I received just by being near her.

We crossed the bridge over the river and wandered along the road through the trees. I found a spot in the middle of a grove that housed the "Mother" tree and I sat down to rest. There were tables and barbecues all formed to surround this tree. The other redwoods grew in a semicircle around its trunk. As I rested in this amphitheater of trees, I overheard a man telling his boys the story of this grove.

The trunk was all that was left of this tree. It was hollow and stood five feet tall and the side was like a small staircase so people could climb into her and explore the inside. As the boys climbed in and out of the tree, the father told them that it was the *Mother Tree.* It was the largest of them all and all the other trees had sprouted from her. As he told them the history I watched the boys raise their heads to follow the tree line. I followed their eyes as they continued up the trees. We all looked straight up and our heads were as far back as they could go.

In an instant it hit me. I am like the mother tree of the redwoods. I have boys growing up around me. My sweetheart has two boys and I have one. They either have or will surpass me with their height, and when we spend time together I'm always surrounded by them. Metaphorically, I have my own grove around me now.

The redwoods gave me a place of refuge to begin again; a place where I could allow my heart to heal and believe that one day I would create that unconditional refuge for others.

In the final chapter of Michael A. Singer's book, *The Untethered Soul; The Journey Beyond Yourself,* he writes, *The beauty is that you can experience this ecstasy. And when you begin to feel this joy, that's when you'll know God's nature. Then nobody will upset or disappoint you. Nothing will create a problem. It will all appear as part of the beautiful dance of creation unfolding before you. Your natural state will get higher and higher. You'll feel love instead of shame. Instead of being unwilling to lift your eyes to the Divine because of what you've said or done, you'll see the Divine as a place of unconditional refuge.*

Contemplate this, and let go of the idea of a judgmental God. You have a loving God. In truth, you have love itself for a God. And love cannot do other than love. Your God is in ecstasy and there's nothing you can do about it. And if God is in ecstasy, I wonder what he sees when He looks at you?

I was so struck by this passage and the peace I felt from reading it I immediately wrote an affirmation right below it in the book:

Beloved Son. When we find each other, or you find me, we will be in a place of unconditional refuge, prompted by my deep desire for my wholeness and your desires that you hold dear.

Today I have this place of refuge for us in my heart and home. I have not physically had contact with my son, yet. I see us both on our own paths and in time, whether it is on this plane of existence or the next, we will meet again. *Peace* comes from this belief.

After we finished our hike through the woods and journeyed back to our campsite, we set out our snacks of fruit, nuts, and cheeses. I got out our deck of cards so we could play our favorite game, rummy. I was in the magic space and won all but one game. I had my sweetheart, food, the music of the river, and the aroma of the redwoods with me.

The smells of food being cooked by families and the sounds of the children at play used to be crushing. Today I carry the sweet memories of my son's toddler years while visiting our favorite place and the bitter part has faded away.

After we finished playing I opened a journal I had brought with me. This was the original journal that I started writing in years prior to writing this book. I reread stories that I wrote and cried for the woman that was so devastated and hurting. I gave myself the acknowledgement that it *was me and that I am no longer her.* Practicing to get out of the story is key to living my life fully and enjoying the beauty that surrounds me now.

This was a passage for me. I was still affected by all that had happened but now I stood fully engaged, surrounded and empowered by the grace of this place.

We packed our things and headed home. We reached the outskirts of the next little town at dinnertime and we had an hour or more to go before we reached home. I suggested we stop at a place that had sentimental value for me. The last time I was there was when I had received the news that my mother had passed away. At the time I knew she was close to passing and I was already on my way to see her. This was several years before and in that period of time I had healed many things in my life.

When we got to the restaurant we found it had closed. This place had been around for decades and I was surprised to see it was no longer in business. So we drove around the corner and made our way through the neighborhood.

As we passed a brightly lit hippie-style restaurant, I suggested we stop and have a look. I'd seen it once before many years ago. It was the kind of place that had a great following and history to it. The restaurant was packed with a joy-filled exuberance. It was a historic home that had been converted to a restaurant. The whole front of the building was floor-to-ceiling windows that looked onto the street and another grove of redwoods. I decided that we should stop and make it a celebratory dinner. He asked, "What are we celebrating?" What came to my mind was, *I'm celebrating it all!* Every high and low, every challenge and sorrow. I'm celebrating my life! We ordered a big Italian meal unlike what I typically do, and toasted to the sweetness in life.

I made a stop in the ladies room before our long drive home. As I washed my hands in the bathroom I looked to see what hung on the back wall. I finished drying my hands and as my eyesight adjusted I saw the rose print! It was exactly the same print I had at home but the color of the rose at home was yellow. I brought this piece of art from my home in Southern California, given to me as a partial payment from the garage sale I had helped with the day before I left. I'd never seen the same print until that day. I looked up the different meanings of the colors of the roses and what I discovered didn't shock me.

With their optimistic hue and general association with good cheer, yellow roses are the perfect way to toast friends, lift spirits, and send a general wish for well-being.

At the time I received this print I was in desperate need of my spirits being lifted as well as my general well-being.

Suited to reverent occasions, the white rose is a fitting way to honor a friend or loved one in recognition of a new beginning or a farewell. Its pure color conveys respect, pays homage to new starts, and expresses hope for the future.

I felt my mother and all the family members who had passed and their well wishes for my new beginning in this description. I felt the horses I had worked with and their hope for my future.

I'm not shocked but always blown away by the manner in which I receive *God's* messages. My spirits are lifted, and there is an abundance of hope for my future. And for all of this my heart is full.

Reflections: A Place of Peace

I'm certain the peace that I experience is dependent on the practices I participate in. I have come a long way in finding my balance, though I still have a bad day every now and then that comes with the terrain of past loss and trauma.

I mention this for this reason. I may have never ventured along the path of profound healing if I had been told that I might still feel the pain of my past memories from time to time. I think we are naturally reminded of our losses of those we've loved when anniversaries of birthdays and holidays come. But in that same revelation, without the willingness to change, the beauty of my life that was waiting for me would never have been found. Having peace in our lives is attainable and it is a practice.

I found the most formative change by working with horses and I know they will be in my life in some manner for the rest of my days. The most important aspects of my work with them were their compassion, curiosity, and trust for me and out of their example grew self-love, and understanding the importance of being present in the moment.

If peace is something you seek, know that finding activities that bring you peace is core to your practice. My choices have been working and volunteering with horses, yoga, meditation, inspirational books and films, and traveling. I quit working in the business that no longer fed my spirit and starting working in my beauty business again. I cultivate and cherish my friendships that bring out the best.

What are your some of the hobbies you are curious about? Is there a trip you have always wanted to take? Do you have a project you have put on hold and never forgotten about, and is now the time to revisit it? What books, films, or new therapies are you interested in engaging in more? It's your time to reach out, to want more for yourself, to be compassionate toward yourself and your journey. You're here and your life is waiting. Don't miss out on what's waiting for you in the beauty of your healing. Peace be with you.

UPDATE

October 5, 2016

As we were finishing up the final details for this book I received another text from my son.

It read "would you like to meet me sometime?"

"Of course I replied!"

By the time this text came in my son had moved up to the Northern California area to start school.

We changed our meeting times and places several times that week and the reality of our reunion was taking shape. My nerves were high and I could feel his were too. On October fifth my partner and I got in our car and began the drive to the arranged meeting spot.

Through our two hour drive his texts continued to change. I could feel his fear and doubts and I was on edge and my mind raced with every conceivable emotion. I tried to reassure myself that I am the Mom, he is the grown up son, and we were both scared and nervous, but willing to meet after eight years.

He initially said he had class starting at 3:30; it was now 3:25. Was he going to show up?

I walked into the sun, in the open parking lot, standing by myself, scanning the passing cars.

I stood unafraid, unapologetic, thinking to myself "I've waited eight years. Eight years!"

As I turned to look at my partner standing in the shade I saw his eyes glance at an oncoming car. He turned to me with a smile in his eyes. I read his lips, he said "I think that's him".

I walked back towards my partner and as we stood together I saw a tall handsome young man walk towards us. I refocused my eyes on this young man. I recognized him from the pictures on the internet. I knew his face; I've known it for eighteen years...*it was my son*!

We spent the next several hours eating, talking, being together in a peace that *truly* does surpass all understanding!

WONDER AND BEAUTY
RESOURCE GUIDE

I did not get to where I am today all by myself. I've had assistance from guides, mentors, and women healers. I've gone through several personal growth programs. In my fragile beginning, I met a shaman healer and we shared a transcendent experience. I was her first client and she introduced me to the power and compassion of the wounded healer as she carefully cut the energetic ties that bound me to my past. She gently led me on my path to the transformation that I live today. Her name is Joy and she exemplifies every bit of this word. She's a Woman's Wisdom Coach and Energetic Healer and Initiated Shaman Mesa Carrier. Learn more about Joyful Living with Joy Brugh at joybrugh.com.

Years ago, in Hawaii, I stopped to pick something up at a shop and met the manager. I was coming down with a bladder infection and in the past these infections sometimes led to a hospital visit. Janet told me she was an acupuncturist and would come and give me a treatment that included aromatherapy after her shift. She saved me from a hospital visit. Today she spends her time as a Holistic Health Designer and yoga instructor, helping people discover new ways of living their lives as healthy and whole human beings. Learn more at www.janetmeredith.net and www.purelivingboutique.com.

In a weekend women's workshop titled The Wonder of Being, I was inspired by the message that we are meant to live our lives with wonder and joy. This was a supportive environment guided by a clinically trained therapist and certified equine specialist. I was no longer living in my survival patterns, but honoring myself with compassion and curiosity. The Wonder of Being workshop had a beautiful mix of expressive arts and equine-guided therapy. I loved the vision board I created, as it is a continuing aid in the unfolding of my dreams today.

Learn more at nancyflambert.com.

I found a place called The Life Healing Center in Santa Fe, New Mexico. I no longer wanted to live with the obstruction of pain and grief. I wanted to finally get to the heart of what was keeping me in that soul-crushing condition. I wanted to be healthy and free again. I received love, compassion, and many answers there. Learn more at life-healing.com.

These divine interactions with healers and teachers were placed perfectly on my path so that I could experience the transformational grace and beauty of loving myself into wholeness. You can too.

The following resources have helped me to heal and grow:

Books/Audiobooks

The God Memorandum by Og Mandino
A Return to Love by Marianne Williamson
Left to Tell by Immaculée Ilibagiza
Anatomy of the Spirit by Caroline Myss
On Becoming Fearless...in Love, Work, and Life by Arianna Huffington
The Shack by Wm. Paul Young
Eat Pray Love by Elizabeth Gilbert
You Can Heal Your Life by Louise Hay
Inspiration: Your Ultimate Calling by Wayne Dyer
Dying to Be Me by Anita Moorjani
The Untethered Soul by Michael A. Singer
Jesus Calling by Sarah Young
The Gifts of Imperfection by Brené Brown

Third Time Lucky by Pasha Hogan
Soul Catcher by Kathy and Amy Eldon
Finding Purpose in Your Pain by V. Gilbert Beers
Brother André: The Wonder Man of Mount Royal by Henri-Paul Bergeron
Brother André: All He Could Do Was Pray by Boniface Hanley
Even Silence Has an End by Ingrid Betancourt
Unbroken by Laura Hillenbrand
Wild: From Lost to Found on the Pacific Crest Trail by Cheryl Strayed
Unstoppable by Nick Vujicic
The Divine Matrix: Bridging Time, Space, Miracles, and Belief by Gregg Braden
Something More: Excavating Your Authentic Self by Sarah Ban Breathnach
Goddesses Never Age by Christiane Northrup
Loveability by Robert Holden Ph.D.
The Mind Body Code by Dr. Mario Martinez
Angels of Abundance by Doreen Virtue and Grant Virtue
The Motivation Manifesto by Brendon Burchard
The Impersonal Life by Joseph S. Benner
Daily Love by Mastin Kipp
I Can See Clearly Now by Wayne Dyer
Way of the Horse: Equine Archetypes for Self-Discovery by Linda Kohanov

Films

You Can Heal Your Life: The Movie by Louise Hay
Buck - Buck Brannaman documentary by Cedar Creek Productions
Dreamer by DreamWorks Pictures
Secretariat by Walt Disney Pictures
Facing the Giants by Sherwood Pictures
The Shift by Hay House
The King's Speech by The Weinstein Company

ACKNOWLEDGEMENTS

The production of this book and my message of love and reunion haven't happened single-handedly. Without the care, assistance, and premonitions of some friends, *Wonder and Beauty* would not exist.

I've wanted to write a book and be a published author for many years. I co-wrote a book decades ago, but that book was never published. I let life get in the way and after many attempts to get it published I shelved it. At that time, my dear friend who had supported me and co-written the book with me said that "the next one" would be on me. She couldn't have been more correct. I don't know if it was as much a premonition as it was a statement, but Colleen Rita Harmon made that declaration to me a few years before she passed away in 2007. She was my best friend and I know she's laughing that hearty laugh of hers right now with delight in her eyes and a song in her heart. Thank you dear friend, for all you did for me in this realm and the next in order to see this come to pass. I can feel that you're proud as hell for me and I miss you like crazy.

To the man and partner in my life. I thank God every day for the synchronicity that brought us together. My darling Dave, I thank you for your presence and your unceasing willingness to know me, love me, and please me in ways I could only have imagined. Your talents and intuition helped me consider new ways to see this book take shape. You are my soul mate and best friend. I am truly one of the luckiest women on earth and I love you dearly.

For my son. Though our story isn't a fairy tale ... *yet*, you are the love of my life, always have been, always will be. From the moment your cheek touched mine in the delivery room my life changed forever. I knew love, saw it, and was so fortunate to hold it every day we were together. I would have never experienced how much I could cherish someone had it not been for you. I am a lucky woman and mother.

To Cristal, my beloved Sista. Thank you for your devotion to me and my son. Thank you for the creation of my *Never Give Up Mom* blog *(nevergiveupmom.com)* and all the hours you spent teaching me about computers, writing the first post, and encouraging me to take the steps to reconnect with my son. You are such a blessing to me and so many. I am truly fortunate to call you my dear and beloved friend. I love you.

To my parents who raised me and taught me what staying the course looks like. Your commitment to nurturing me and loving me taught me a lot in the face of adversity. I am grateful that I learned so much from both of you. I know you're proud of me and wish me well. I love you both.

To my brother James who taught me that to have a consciousness filled with compassion is a strong suit. I know we didn't share a lot of time growing up together, but I know your heart and I believe you know mine. Thank you for teaching me to reach out and help others in need of a strong voice and advocate. I love you, James.

To my birth father Lee and the entire Kenniston family, thank you for welcoming me into Kenniston tribe. Thank you for always reminding me that I have a home with you if ever I need it. And thank you for showering me with the Kenniston sense of humor you all seem to possess. I love you.

For Dayle and Collin Henry. I am grateful for your love and care in the midst of the toughest years of my life. I want you both to know there will always be a special place in my heart for the two of you, and I don't know how I would have made it through those dark days without you. I love you.

Thank you to my sisters from the Hixon family. I always feel your love and adoration even though we're miles apart and our time together has been brief. I appreciate your support and care every time I hear from you. I love you.

To the Gosman family—Amy, Delia, Bella and Angus. You gave me your hearts and home. You fed me and offered me your friendship and care. You have always supported my son and me in the worst of conditions and times. Thank you all for your kindness; for these things and many more, I will always be grateful for you. Karen and Elaine, your spirits have been with me from the time I wrote my first book to the creation of this one. I've always felt your well wishes and torment as you knew mine. You are both the kind of women I'm so proud to know and am so lucky to call you my spirit guides as well as friends. Thank you for all your years of prayer. I love you both.

To Eva, my devoted friend and "mother," thank you being my first mentor and teaching me through your example to never give up or give in. Your tenacious demeanor taught me well and your generosity of spirit is enviable. Thank you for standing by me in my dark years and nursing my spirit back to health. I am a very lucky woman to have known you and I'll forever be grateful to you for the examples of strength and perseverance you taught me. I wouldn't be what I am today without you. I love you.

To my friend Danitza Levasseur. Because of your belief in me, I was able to move forward through this unfathomable story. Thank you for your unending support for my son and me, and for your effort to help us reunite. For these things and so many more I will always be grateful to you. I love you, Dani.

To my editor Beverly Ehrman. I knew in the first few minutes of speaking with you that I had not only met the right editor, but a sage. I wasn't about to shelve this book, and because of you I knew that would never happen. Thank you for your earnest nature and your steady hand. This project meant more to me than any undertaking I've done and you knew that. You delivered more than what you promised and at record speed. Thank you for taking my story and polishing it to a beautiful finish. You are what every writer dreams of and much more. What an honor and joy to have worked with you.

For my friends Michele and Buck. Thank you for your support and time these past two years. Your feedback was invaluable to me and just knowing you're available day and night has been comforting. I know you're both rooting for me and the book. I truly love and appreciate you both.

Valerie Valentine. You are a gift from God. Sitting with you through the first eighteen days of my stay altered my journey. I thought my tears would never end, but you knew better. Thank you for being by my side as I went into the deepest parts of my story and emerged forever changed. You are my trusted advisor and confident of the highest order. I am so fortunate to know you. I love you.

For Pasha Hogan. Thank you for the care you took with me when I came to you. You are a true goddess in every sense of the word. Your tender and gentle nature helped me to morph into the woman I am today and your display of gentle strength is admirable. You gave me the template to follow through this healing journey and for all of this I'm grateful. Thank you for walking with me through my barren start and showering me with your creative energy and love for yoga.

For Dr. Nancy Freitas Lambert. It's truly impossible to put my gratitude for you into a few words. When I came to you I was a shattered woman I thought beyond repair. Never did I dream I'd live the life I'm living today. You have more than the capacity to hold the space for others healing while gently reminding them that they are worth it and their lives do matter. You're a light in a complicated mental health care system. You embody and represent the other side to depression and hopelessness. You gave me the time and space to become curious about living my life in wonder, and as a result I walk with respect for myself and I stand tall in my truth. I have crossed over that bridge of my past thanks to you and your herd of horses, and I will forever be grateful for the time I've spent with you.

ABOUT THE AUTHOR

Charla Miller is the founder of *BeautyHealsYou.com--* a website and blog that integrates the concept of emotional and physical beauty. As a makeup and skin care expert she shows women how to take care of their skin and the power of their beauty through her artistry services. The blog is a resource that introduces other integrative healing practices, skin care and makeup tips and inspiring events.

Charla started as a makeup and hair artist in Hollywood and she continues to work in commercials, advertising campaigns, as an artist in global cosmetic brands and weddings in the San Francisco Bay area and beyond.

She is also the creator of the website, *NeverGiveUpMom.com.* She began writing in 2012 as a way to communicate her love and commitment to her stolen son. The site has a global following with the desire to inspire other parents and family members to start believing in the possibility of reunion even in the midst of their child's absence and gives voice to the power to carry on and ultimately reunite.

When she isn't busy in her artistry and writing endeavors she takes every opportunity to immerse herself in the beauty of nature and volunteer with Michael Muir's Access Adventure and his beloved herd of horses. Her mission is to continue to become a better horsewoman and share the healing nature of horses with others.

If you would like Charla to lead a Beauty Heals You Workshop, book a private artistry appointment, or speak at your conference, please contact her at charlamiller.com.

The author communing with Tango in Santa Fe, New Mexico.

Printed in the United States
By Bookmasters